Being Friends

Peter Levin was born in London in 1936. He
trained as a physicist, and did research in
industry for four years, living and working in
Harlow new town. During that time, his
interest shifted away from physics to people,
politics, and the subject of how government
bodies take decisions, and he took up
research into new town planning, first as a
civil servant and then at a university. He is
now a university lecturer. He has an ex-wife
and a son, now independent, and enjoys a
warm and relaxed relationship with both of
them.

Among his pleasures in life are working
with students, enquiring into decision-
making, fighting campaigns of various kinds,
walking on hills, folk dancing (the kind that
involves a lot of energetic leaping about),
adventures in foreign countries, and – above
all – his friends. He wrote *Being Friends* after
they had helped him through a deeply
distressing period in his life.

PETER LEVIN

Being Friends

Collins
FOUNT PAPERBACKS

First published in Great Britain in 1987
by Fount Paperbacks, London

Copyright © Peter Levin 1987

Typeset by V & M Graphics Ltd, Aylesbury, Bucks
Made and printed in Great Britain by
William Collins Sons & Co. Ltd, Glasgow

To each of my friends,
with love and gratitude

Contents

The subj...........................ry difficult
subject t...........about,........................hat *feelings*
play in o...................of f................e communicate ou................................peaking and
writing......................................convey the
nature of these................................But it seems
important to try. In these days, when...............e than ever are
living on their own or as single parents, we are increasingly
looking to friends for the support and pleasures that in the past
we would have sought from our families. Even if you are
married or "partnered", the chances are – especially if you are
a woman – that you depend on friends for some things, and
recognize the fact.

But friendships not only provide support and pleasures, they
create difficulties too. They may be a bit less complex than
some other relationships, like family ones, but none the less
they are sometimes demanding, sometimes unpredictable, and
cannot be taken for granted. They present us with problems –
for example, if we get into a situation where one of us is doing
all the giving and the other all the taking, or if we have difficulty
fitting them into the rest of our lives. Is it possible to have both
a strong, committed relationship with your spouse or partner
and strong, platonic friendships with other people, as an
individual in your own right? Or do you feel obliged to share all
your friends, operating as a couple all the time and dropping
people that you don't both get on with? If you are facing any
problems like these, I hope that something in this book will

"resonate" with you, and help you to clarify the problem and deal constructively with it.

This book has many limitations. It is written by a white, heterosexual male in his late forties, who is neither a poet nor a psychologist. It deals only with friendships between two individuals, and not among groups of people, because I have only limited experience of the latter. It is one person's attempt to make sense of his experience of friendship, and to generalize from it and what he knows of the experiences of his own friends and others. My qualifications are, I suppose, that I have some worthwhile friendships to my name, and some failures too; that I have had friends to thank for seeing me through some very low times and sharing in some very high ones; and that I am a feeling, thinking, human being, like everybody else.

My friends have participated in a very real way in the making of this book, not only by virtue of the fact that it draws on our shared experience, but in a practical way too, by commenting on successive drafts, testing my arguments, challenging my ideas, putting forward their own. The writing and rewriting of it has thus been a very rewarding enterprise for me, not least because I have learned such a lot from and with them. I am delighted to acknowledge my debt to them. Notwithstanding which, I do of course take full responsibility for everything that I say and advocate in these pages, and for anything that I should have put in but haven't.

As you can see, the book is divided into three parts. Part One is focused on three general but important questions: What is friendship? Do we "need" friends? Who are our friends? In trying to supply answers to these questions, I draw quite a lot on books that other people have written. In Part Two, I discuss in turn what I see as the "ingredients" of friendship – the essentials that make friendships work. What I'm trying to do here is to formulate some ideas about friendship, drawing on my own experience and that of other people, some of which I've been told about and some of which I've read about. And in

Part Three, I try to use those ideas to make suggestions about things we can do to create friendships and make friendships work better.

PART ONE

Friendship: Some Questions

1

What Is Friendship?

There are no single or 'right' answers to the questions "What is friendship?" and "What is a friend?" "Friendship" and "friend" are words which different people use in different ways. I might describe as my friend someone who went to school with me and who now lives near me, so that we quite often see each other in the street and say hello and ask "How are you?" Or I might rate as a friend someone who works alongside me, whose company I enjoy and who enjoys mine, and with whom I go out for a drink every Friday lunchtime. Or I might use the word "friend" in the way that I actually prefer to do, to denote someone who is special to me, as I am to them, the two of us having very few if any secrets from each other and sharing our deepest joys and fears: other people might talk about "real" friends or "close" friends when they mean this sort of relationship. In this book I shall be using the words "friend" and "friendship" in this third sense. So when you see them you can always take it for granted that I do mean a relationship that would qualify as "real" or "close" – at the other extreme to a mere acquaintanceship.

At the heart of any friendship is the fact that the friends have feelings about each other. What can we say about these feelings?

If we look up the word "friend" in a dictionary we will find it defined using other words such as "liking", "affection", "loyalty", "benevolence". And these in turn are defined using more words: "affection" is equated with "fondness" and "tenderness", for example. But then to be "fond" of someone is to have a "liking" for them, and so we go round and round in circles: unless any of these words is particularly significant or meaningful for us, this exercise doesn't get us much further. Let's try a different approach. If we were to ask a number of people what feelings they have when they're with their friends, we would probably get answers like these:

"We care about each other."

"We enjoy seeing one another and going out together."

"I don't feel so alone knowing I can just pick up the phone and have a chat."

"It's really good being able to talk to someone you can trust and feel comfortable with, especially if you're angry or upset about something."

"We have a lot of laughs together."

"You get a really warm feeling being with someone who understands exactly what you're trying to say, even if you can't say it very well."

"We've seen each other through all sorts of times, good as well as bad, so we have a sort of fellow-feeling towards each other."

"Friends accept you as you are, not as they want you to be."

"Friends make you feel good about yourself."

Do you recognize any of these feelings? If you do, you'll know what I mean by friendship – an amalgam of feelings like these, not in any fixed proportions (probably no two friendships are exactly alike), but experienced mutually by two people who are friends with each other. If we want to sum up these feelings using single words, then no doubt "caring", "affection", "loyalty", "fondness" and "tenderness" will do very well. But they leave something out, I think. These words are only about the feelings that one person "directs" towards another: they don't reflect the feelings of the person who's on the receiving end, or the fact that friendship is a two-way relationship.

What words are there that sum up the feelings that we have as a result of being on the *receiving* end of someone else's caring, affection, etc., or as the result of *sharing* (participating) in a friendship? Unfortunately the English language is terribly deficient in such words (which perhaps says something about our culture and society), so mostly we shall have to make do with rather clumsy expressions. Let me make some suggestions. What we experience as recipients in our friendships are feelings of being cared about and cherished, of being accepted and respected, of being trusted and able to trust, perhaps of being close to and "comforted" by our friend. As to the feelings we have that come from sharing in a friendship – the feelings that embrace mutuality – expressions that come to mind are warming to each other, togetherness, comradeship, and "withness", a sense of being at one with each other. The word "rapport" seems to me an appropriate one to sum up these feelings. Thus, to care for someone and feel cared-about by them, and so on with someone, and also feel rapport with them, is to know what friendship is, to know that friends are treasures without which our lives would be poorer.

When I look at my own friendships and those of people I know, they strike me as being made up of several "ingredients". These are present in different proportions in different friendships, but all of them seem to be present to some degree. Here is a list. I describe them only briefly here because each gets a chapter to itself later on.

1. Friends are attracted to each other. Quite what the forces of attraction are, and why we are attracted to one person but not another, is something of a mystery, but there can be no doubt that these forces exist.
2. Friends have rapport with one another, a feeling of oneness and mutual warmth. This requires a number of the ingredients listed below, but in particular it requires empathy, the ability to sense and understand another person's feelings, and experience them almost as if they were one's own.

3. Friends reach out to one another, each from his or her own "base". Each has some "sense of self", a sense of his or her own identity, of who they are, and each recognizes the same thing in the other.

4. Friends accept and respect each other. They welcome each other, invite each other into their company, take each other seriously, treat each other as equals, and allow each other to be himself or herself.

5. Friends take on obligations to one another. They allow each other to have expectations of them – that they can be depended on, that the friendship will not suddenly cease to exist.

6. Friends care about and cherish each other. They have feelings towards each other, of a warm and positive kind, like affection and loyalty, and also feelings in response to each other – they feel that they matter and are valued, for example.

7. Friends trust one another. Without trust, people will not confide in one another, nor will they have any grounds for expecting that the other will be there when needed, which is important to friendship.

8. Friends give to and receive from each other. They give not out of social obligation, or a guilty conscience, or the desire to get something in return, but out of goodwill. To paraphrase Aristotle, they wish each other good for his or her own sake.

9. Friends talk and listen to one another, and confide in one another. They reveal their emotional selves – their "child within" – to each other. On my definition, a relationship between two people is not a friendship, although there may be a bond between them, if they don't confide in one another at this level.

10. Friends do things together. They meet, spend time in each other's company, often join in some physical or brain-using activity together. They share in the doing and the

decision-making. Even if they don't meet so frequently or regularly as once they did, their shared history is important to them.

A number of things follow from all this. First, friendship is multi-dimensional. It is a mixture of doing, of exercising abilities, of having attitudes and feelings. It is not a simple phenomenon but a rich and complex one, and no two friendships will ever be exactly the same as each other. Second, friendships are mutual, reciprocal relationships. They involve shared experiences and two-way interaction. As Ralph Waldo Emerson said, "The only way to have a friend is to be one" (*Friendship*). In this sense, you are equals, even if the relationship is based on your complementing each other rather than on the similarities between you. Third, the relationship is psychologically and "politically" a comparatively straightforward and uncomplicated one. By comparison to the relationship that most of us have with our parents or children, or with the person whom we share a bed with, there are relatively few deep psychological processes going on in the background – so you aren't playing roles like mother-figure and father-figure for each other – and relatively few links of obligation between you: there are *some*, as I've said, but they aren't such that you are able – nor do you try – to put great pressure on each other to get your own way, for example. (This is not to say that you and your partner, child or parents can't be friends, that family relationships and friendship are mutually exclusive. What I *would* argue is that if you and your partner are to be friends as well as partners, you must get the psychological knots out of the way and learn not to play power games on one another.) And fourth, there is continuity to friendship. It existed in the past, even if only the recent past; it exists now; and we have expectations that it will go forward – perhaps indefinitely, perhaps not – into the future. It follows that friendship is a *dynamic* relationship. It is not a fixed thing, a status quo. It requires to be maintained in being, to be reaffirmed, through the continuing criss-crossing and weaving together of our lives.

A final point that follows from my list of the "ingredients" of friendship will remind us of what is left out as well as what is included. I am defining "friendship" in its platonic sense – that is to say, without any sexual connotation, such as we bring in when we talk about "my boyfriend" or "my girlfriend" (although women sometimes refer to their women friends as "girlfriends"). I don't want to press this distinction too far, though. I suspect that the forces of attraction that underlie many close, comradely friendships between people who are sexually compatible – heterosexual people of the opposite sex, or homosexual people of the same sex – do have something in common with the forces that underlie sexual relationships. Perhaps, indeed, there is actually an element of sexual attraction underlying many friendships that are ostensibly platonic and comradely. Even though the relationship never becomes a physically sexual one, sexual attraction can give it a "spark" that other relationships lack.

2

Do We "Need" Friends?

In the previous chapter I attempted to answer the question "What is friendship?" by giving examples of the feelings that people say they have about their friends. If you look back at them, you will see that they all suggest that friends are good for you, that to have friends is nice and pleasurable and rewarding. In the chapters that follow I shall try to spell out and explain these "pay-offs" in some detail. But do we actually *need* friends? By which I mean, is there any sense in which having friends is actually essential to our well-being?

One approach to answering this question is to ask another: what happens to people who are friendless? The answer we find is that being friendless seems to be associated with certain unhappy states of mind, such as depression. Dorothy Rowe, in her book *Depression: The Way out of Your Prison*, writes: "If you want to find your way out of the prison of depression, you need friends." She stresses the mutuality of friendship and also the importance of a friend as someone in whom you can confide. "In confiding in another person we are, in effect, telling our tale. Each of us has a story, the story of our life, and as we tell that story, or just part of it, we know that our life has significance, at least in our eyes and the eyes of the person who listens ... In listening to another person's story we are, in effect, bearing witness to that person's existence, courage, suffering and pain." Without another person to bear witness in this way, it may be very difficult not to become depressed, or at the very least insecure, and retreat into a lonely world of our own, perhaps becoming one of those "odd" people who can be seen holding imaginary conversations, talking out loud by themselves. There is evidence that many people who are troubled and depressed don't in fact have anyone to confide in, to tell their story to.

The importance of "self-disclosure" is underlined by Sidney Jourard in *The Transparent Self*: "Self-disclosure is a symptom of personality health *and* a means of ultimately achieving a healthy personality ... People's selves stop growing when they repress them ... Every maladjusted person is a person who has not made himself known to another human being and in consequence does not know himself. Nor can he be himself. More than that, he struggles actively to avoid becoming known by another human being."

Quite a few studies have been made of the effects on people of bereavement, isolation and hospitalization, and of the loneliness, lack of support and so on, that result from them. Some of these studies are cited by Steve Duck, a psychologist, in his book *Friends, For Life*. He argues that "loneliness or isolation is important psychologically precisely because it deprives people of their psychological bench-marks and anchor points: they lose the stability provided by the chance to compare their own reactions to life with the reactions of other people that they know, like and respect." Why, though, do these "other people" have to be friends rather than, say, just other members of the community where you live, or members of your own family? The answer seems to be that members of our local community, like sympathetic strangers on long-distance trains, don't share with us a *history* of doing things together, of talking and listening, of caring and cherishing, giving and receiving, so we have little basis for trusting or having expectations of one another, or for a genuine dialogue as opposed to getting things off our respective chests. On the other hand, so far as members of our own family are concerned, the psychological complexity of our relationships with them and the intricate web of obligations and expectations in a family is liable to make it difficult to achieve the openness and mutuality that we experience with our friends. Indeed, one of the most valuable things that friends do for one another is to help in coping with the tensions created *within* the family. This is certainly true of teenagers, and probably of the majority of adult women too. Luise Eichenbaum and Susie Orbach, in *What do Women Want?*, argue that "because women friends are able to give each other emotional nurturance and contact, women can feel 'fed' by their friends and not look only to their men for fulfilment. This brings less pressure to men in relationships. In other words, girlfriends help each other to stay in heterosexual relationships."

Evidence of the value of the support that women give one another, and also of the connection between having friends and mental health, comes from a survey by Carol Parris in South London. Of the forty women whom she interviewed, ten had no close friends at all, while most had only one close friend. Many had close relationships with their mother and/or sisters. One woman said: "If I stopped seeing my friends I'd be back on the lonely trail, wouldn't I? If we all stopped being friends, I'd be back how I was before, back to the depression stage. I find talking to my friends can be a lot easier than talking to my husband. Let's face it, he's a smashing bloke but he can't understand ... He's at work all day so he can't understand the situation. Where if you speak to the girls they're more sympathetic. They're in the same boat as me. They've all got young children at home, and if I feel a bit down about something I can talk to them about it and I find I feel a lot better." The women whom Carol Parris interviewed spoke enthusiastically of the way in which friendships with other women eased personal worries and frequently became substitutes for visits to the doctor. And it is clear, from what her interviewees said, that visiting the doctor is a very inadequate substitute for having friends.

Finally, the extent to which we ourselves *feel* that we need friends is bound to depend on our personality. If, say, your childhood was marked by periodic humiliations or rejections, or by insensitive treatment generally, you may have entered on adult life desperately wanting to be liked – a feeling that you identify as a "need" for friends. It may actually be essential that you achieve this aim, in that psychological harm may result if you don't. (So it would be a need as I defined it in the opening paragraph of this chapter, too.) The problem may be, though, that your life up to now has left you with a poorly developed sense of self, which may make it very difficult for you to make and sustain friendships. I shall say something about this problem in the chapter on "Sense of Self", and something about how to tackle it in Part Three. Meanwhile, I conclude that we *do* need friends: they are essential to our mental health and stability, they are essential if we are to experience fulfilment in our lives, and they are essential if we are to function competently in our many "interactions" with other people – at home, at work, at play, indeed everywhere.

3

Who Are Our Friends?

Quite a lot of research has been done into "patterns" of friendship, by psychologists, sociologists, social anthropologists, and psychotherapists. Unfortunately the specialists in one discipline tend to ignore the work that's been done in others, so the overall picture is very disjointed. In this chapter I want to highlight and draw together some of the findings about friendship patterns, and have a shot at explaining them, drawing on commonsense as well as whatever bit of the social sciences is relevant.

So who *are* our friends? According to psychologist Steve Duck, "Friendships are usually formed with people of the same religion and socio-economic level, who have a similar job, similar background, similar educational history, similar level of income, similar recreational interests, and similar racial origins." No reference here, you may notice, to any difference between men and women, or to friendships between men and women. Michael Argyle, in *The Psychology of Interpersonal Behaviour*, mentions a number of studies of what friends do together, and these show variations according to age, social class and sex. "Between adolescence and the age of twenty-five friends may spend hours a day together; in middle age they may only meet once a month, family and social contacts at work seeming to have replaced friendships. Middle-aged people also find it more difficult to make new friends than when they were younger ... In the early 1970s, working-class people in Britain met acquaintances in specific settings, such as at work, the pub, the club or church, but did not usually see them in more than one setting and tended not to ask them home. They had fewer

25

friends in the middle-class sense, while kin were more important to them and did get asked home, or asked themselves." As to sex: "Women friends *talk*, drink coffee, disclose confidences and provide social support; men friends play squash, help each other and in a number of ways *do* things together – there is less disclosure and intimacy, though men often drink together and talk about work. As well as having fewer intimate friendships, men have fewer friends altogether, especially in middle age." It is interesting that Argyle too makes no mention of friendships between men and women. "The reason for these sex differences is not agreed upon: it could be male fear of homosexuality, male competitiveness at work and sport, or the fact" – ? – "that work contacts meet the same needs, or it may be that women have greater need of social support and greater skills at providing it." This is a rather perfunctory speculation: it makes no reference to the possibility that people want friends for other reasons besides meeting needs – pleasure and enjoyment, for example.

Perhaps the most interesting and valuable study of friendship patterns has been made by a social anthropologist, Elizabeth Bott. It is described in her book *Family and Social Network*, first published in 1957. She found that the friendships you have will reflect your social class, the neighbourhood you live in and whether you have lived there all your life, as well as the pattern of friendships that your parents had. Thus, at one extreme were working-class neighbourhoods with "close-knit networks" – that is to say, where many of your friends, neighbours and relatives know each other as well as knowing you – and where husbands and wives have their own networks, which are often quite separate, made up of different people. In these families there is not only "segregation" between the parents' networks, but also between those of parents and children. The children grow up in single-sex "peer groups", and develop a strong sense of solidarity with one another – especially strong among adolescent boys. When boys start work they don't have to move away from the neighbourhood, so the friendships of adolescence can be continued into adulthood to form an adult peer group. This consists of friends, some of whom are neighbours, some of whom are relatives, and some of whom may be workmates. These male networks are balanced by female networks of relatives and sometimes friends, and the pattern continues after marriage, thus reproducing the parents' pattern, although it seemed that a girl's relationships with her friends were of great importance until she had her first child, after which she would probably turn more and more to relatives. If she lived in a homogeneous neighbourhood, she would probably turn also to neighbours, who can provide the little bits of help and assistance that she did not need before.

At the other extreme were families with very loose-knit networks – i.e. the people that they knew did not meet each other independently of them. These families were likely to be middle class, with husbands and wives sharing the same, loose-knit network, and with less "social distance" between parents and children. So parents usually knew about their children's friends and what the children and their friends did together. Peer groups did exist, but weren't so cut off from the family. Middle-class families were also more likely to move around geographically, which had the effect of training children to expect their friendships to be interrupted. They were also liable to attend schools in different neighbourhoods from the one where they lived, and to proceed through school and higher education leaving a trail of friendships behind them. All these factors, Elizabeth Bott reckoned, worked together to develop in middle-class children the skills necessary for operating a joint relationship and a loose-knit network. "The ability to make friends is an important aspect of these skills." During adolescence children might combine intense attachment to peer groups with relationships with members of the opposite sex, but soon the "mating pairs" separate themselves out, and pursuit of careers disperses the peer groups. Friends are "trimmed" so that they can be joint, with the husband probably dominating this process. The intense relationships of late adolescence remain as reminders of the continuity of one's individual identity, or of the couple's identity if the friend is a mutual one. "But most 'mutual' friends were originally the friends of one or other spouse, and the mutuality of the friendship is somewhat precarious. These intense identity-giving friends tend to be conveniently absent so that they do not threaten conjugal loyalty. Brief visits add spice to life; constant residence near such a friend is somewhat awkward. Henceforth new friendships are joint, but very much diminished in intensity. Joint acquaintanceship succeeds individual friendships." Perhaps middle-class children *do* develop friend-making skills, as Elizabeth Bott says, but they do not seem to make use of them later on in life: she herself quotes a study which shows that middle-class people make only a few close friendships after marriage.

Between these two extremes of friendship patterns there is a vast range of intermediate ones, about which we don't know very much. One thing does seem clear, though. Someone who grows up in a long-resident family in a stable working-class neighbourhood, but is then uprooted by a move in search of work, or by a local council scheme of "slum clearance" and redevelopment, or who stays put while others move away, may not have learned the skills necessary to make friends in their new environment. And if they cannot acquire these skills, possibly rather late in life, it is surely all too likely that they could be very vulnerable to depression and other kinds of mental ill-health.

More recently, a survey in Britain (cited by Mary Ingham, in *Men*) suggested that fifty per cent of men in this country have no friends, apart from work colleagues. In her own survey of nearly a hundred men in their mid-thirties, most of whom had attended grammar schools, nearer eighty per cent admitted that they had no close friends. "The friendships they did have centred around work, and it was a general rule not to see too much of these people outside work and never to confide in them." Mary Ingham makes no reference to joint – i.e. family – friends, but her findings suggest that even if husbands and wives have joint friends, the husbands don't feel them to be close friends. So if middle-class men do learn friend-making skills in their childhood, either those skills don't get used or they're good for making superficial friendships but not close ones.

In the USA, a study of the friendship patterns of men and women has been carried out by Lillian B. Rubin, who interviewed over two hundred men and women – married, divorced, and single – who ranged in age from twenty-five to fifty-five and came from all walks of life. She reports her findings in her book *Intimate Strangers*. Women have more friendships (as distinct from collegial relationships or work-mates) than men, and there are marked differences in the content and quality of their friendships. "Over two-thirds of the single men couldn't name a best friend. Of those who could, it was much more likely to be a woman than a man who held that place in their lives. In contrast, over three-quarters of the single women had no problem in identifying a best friend, and almost always that person was a woman. Among those who were married, far more men than women named a spouse as a best friend, their most trusted confidante, and/or the one they would be most likely to turn to in emotional distress. For the married women, it was a strikingly different picture. Even when a woman did name her husband to one or more of these roles, it was never exclusively his, as was most likely to be the case with a man. Most women identified at least one, usually more, trusted friends to whom they could turn in a troubled moment, and they spoke openly and ardently about the importance of these relationships in their lives ... Even when a man claimed a best friend, the two shared little about the interior of their lives and feelings. It wasn't unusual, for example, to hear a man say that he didn't know his friend's marriage was in serious trouble until he appeared one night asking if he could sleep on the couch. And men who claimed years of close friendship failed to confide their distress at the discovery of a wife's extramarital affair."

On a different tack, Robin Skynner, of the Institute of Family Therapy, describes a demonstration of the unconscious attractions – the "chemistry" – that draw together people whose backgrounds have something in common. You can find this in the book which he wrote with John Cleese – *Families and How to Survive Them*. Complete strangers (actually brand-new trainee therapists) are put in a room together, and asked to choose another person from the group who either makes them think of someone in their family, or, alternatively, gives them the feeling that they would have filled a "gap" in the family. They aren't allowed to speak at all while choosing, but just wander around looking at all the others. When they've all chosen someone – that is, when they're in pairs – they are told to talk together for a time, to see whether they can find out what made them pick each other. They're encouraged to compare their family backgrounds. Next, each couple is asked to choose another couple, to make up foursomes. And then, each foursome is asked to form itself into a family of some kind, the members agreeing with each other what role in the family each of them will take. Then they talk together about what it was in their family backgrounds that led to their decisions. And finally, they report to the whole group what they've discovered – which is invariably that the members of each foursome have a remarkable number of similarities in their family backgrounds, in their family histories, and in their families' attitudes. For example, they might find that all four of them are from families where there was difficulty in sharing affection, or perhaps in expressing anger, or envy; or where there had been a lot of near-incestuous relationships; or where people had always been expected to be optimistic and cheerful. Or they might discover that all four of them had fathers who were away from home during the years when that mattered a lot to them; or that all their families had suffered some big loss or change of a similar kind when they were all at similar ages.

What this exercise shows is that, as John Cleese puts it, "We're carrying around our families with us, somewhere inside us, and we're giving off signals which enable others with similar backgrounds to recognize us." How does this work? According to Robin Skynner, over and above the *changing* emotions which we experience all the time – moods – we all have certain *habitual* emotions or attitudes. These show themselves in our posture, facial expressions, and the typical way we move. "Take a depressive person. He'll tend to slump and slouch and move apathetically. And by virtue of having his face in a depressed expression over the years, he'll develop certain facial lines which we recognize immediately. The same applies to a cheerful fellow who smiles a lot – he'll get laugh lines, and will usually move in a more positive, eager, upright kind of way; somebody a bit manic will move jerkily and seem tense and tend to have rather staring eyes."

While it is true that Robin Skynner's trainees were prompted to look for partners who reminded them of "family", it appears that people may in general be attracted to others who give out similar signals, and indeed may subsequently get on well with them. (Up to a point, at least.) So it could be that insofar as we choose our *friends*, we may choose them on the basis of these signals. So one thing that could determine who our friends are could be similarity of family background, which is certainly consistent with Steve Duck's observation that I quoted at the beginning of this chapter. If our family backgrounds are similar, we might well have religion, racial origins and educational history in common too.

But what explains the differences between the friendship patterns of men and women, and the differences in the quality of men's and women's friendships that Lillian Rubin remarked on? Why is it that women experience "intimacy" with one another whereas all that men have, by and large, is a "bond of understanding" created by "the shared experience of male-ness"? Why do men share all kinds of activities but hardly ever talk about feelings, leading Lillian Rubin to describe their friendships with one another as "emotionally impoverished"? According to several writers, the source of these differences, and also of the problems that men and women have in relating to each other, is to be found in the process by which boys and girls establish their "gender identity" – their sense of being male or female – and their separateness from their mother. To put it briefly, and in my own words: A little boy learns to define himself in opposition to his mother, as being different from her. He becomes accustomed to seeing his relationship with her as a bridge across a divide, and takes this view subcons-ciously with him into other relationships, especially with women, in later life. A little girl, however, learns to define herself as being *the same* as her mother: she absorbs the lesson that to relate to someone is to be close to them, if not to *merge* with them. As a boy grows up, social pressures teach him that he is expected to be independent, to stand on his own two feet, that it is admirable to be "a proper handful". Girls, however, are taught more subtle – and more subservient – ways of relating. From being "Daddy's girl" they go on to learn to make themselves pretty – which means learning to gauge their effect on other people and to measure their success as girls by that effect – and to be sensitive to other people ("What shall we get Daddy for his dinner?") and indeed to protect the ego of the males around her. In other words, boys learn self-affirmation, girls learn relating. Growing up with "peer groups" through childhood and adolescence can reinforce these lessons, and so can the example set by parents in the way that they conduct their relationships and "networks". Yet there are of course differences between social classes, as Elizabeth Bott points out.

In particular, being brought up as a middle-class kid can teach you some skills in making new friends, although the friendships that they help you to form may be only superficial ones.

Who our friends are will inevitably depend also on the society we live in – in particular on the rules and conventions of the particular bit of it, the "milieu", in which we live, work and relate to other people. This milieu provides us with certain opportunities to make friends with various other people, but also puts obstacles in the way of our making friends with yet others. For example, if we belong to an ethnic or religious minority, we may have many opportunities to make friends with fellow members, but encounter strong disapproval if we try to make friends with non-members. The obstacles may also take the form of our own inhibitions: "What would all my left-wing friends say if I became friends with people with posh accents?", asked one of my own friends. And a budding friendship may run into a lot of trouble if other people in the same milieu suspect that the relationship may have or could develop a sexual as well as a comradely dimension. Thus, in some social milieus it may be "not done" for someone who is married or engaged to be seen having an intense and thoughtful conversation – one of those conversations where you're oblivious to what's going on around you – with someone of the opposite sex who isn't a relative. If they do, "people will talk". In other milieus, however, like the middle-class ones of professional occupations (teachers, social workers and so on), there will be much more tolerance, especially if the opportunity for the conversation doesn't look as though it has been furtively contrived. Entrance to some social milieus, and with it opportunities for making friends, may depend crucially on whether you are married or not. For example, getting married may bring you admission to the middle-class world of dinner parties given by couples for other couples, and if your marriage breaks up you may find yourself instantly dropped by people whom you thought were your friends (that's when you find out who your *real* friends are).

The existence of a social barrier to friendships between married men and women (married or unmarried) is testified to by Mary Ingham's finding in her survey of men, that "most men regarded the suggestion that they might have 'female friends' as an attempt to discover whether they had ever been unfaithful to their wives." Perhaps this reflected an inability on the part of those men to imagine having a platonic relationship with a woman, but I suspect that few of the wives concerned would have been happy that their husbands should have female friends. The popular notion that the male is always on the look-out for sex seems to inhibit a man from seeking to be friends with a woman, whether it is actually true in his case or not.

One last study of friendship patterns which deserves a mention here is the one that was made by Ann Whitehead in Herefordshire (England) about ten years ago. (It is described briefly by Dale Spender in her book *Man Made Language*.) Ann Whitehead found that in the community she studied wives were isolated from each other, prevented from talking to each other and thus from making new friendships with others or sustaining old ones. She argues that husbands appear to make bargains which often include that their wives should see less or nothing of their girlfriends. "These links are a threat in that they represent a most dangerous channel of communication. If the wives tell each other about their marriages, this information may be passed on to a husband. Where the first husband is also a drinking companion of the second, this information may be used in pub disclosures." The driving force behind this behaviour of the husbands appears to be the fear that the macho image that they present in the competitive, jousting arena of the pub will be shown to be nothing more than an image, and a false one at that. The explanation of the wives' isolation thus appears to have its roots in the fragility of the male ego, and this is consistent with Robin Skynner's observation that in general women are indeed extraordinarily considerate and protective of the male ego. (Which is not to say that a man may not sometimes feel he can detect an element of condescension on the woman's part.) The difference between rural Herefordshire and urban society seems to be that in the latter men have no option but to trust their wives not to give away domestic secrets: in the rural community, however, they actually use their power to gain that end. If we enquire more deeply and ask what explains the fragility of the male ego, perhaps we have to look for the answer to that early childhood experience of establishing our difference and separateness from our mothers. Do we (that is, men) perhaps experience this as the most crushing rejection of all time, the memory of which we may suppress but of which we can never totally rid ourselves?

It is not only men who form and stick to "peer groups". The past twenty years have seen the setting up in the USA and Britain of countless women's groups – consciousness-raising groups, reading groups, mutual help and support groups. It seems safe to say that people have a built-in tendency or "disposition" to get together with others. This disposition may not come to fruition, if the opportunity doesn't exist or isn't made, but it seems to be there nevertheless. Not only do we gravitate towards others with a similar family background, as Robin Skynner shows, but we seek out others who are in the same boat as we are, facing the same problems, or who have similar attitudes or interests. They tend to see things the same way and to talk the same language – not just English or Greek or whatever or a particular dialect, but in a cultural or political sense. Here then seems to be another basic drive that helps to explain friendship patterns.

In conclusion, it is necessary, I think, to issue a warning against attaching too much significance to the reported findings of the studies that I have mentioned. Asking people about friendships is a fraught business. We *claim* friends rather than just count them up as we can our children or our TV sets, we use different criteria to judge whether someone is our friend or not, and some of us doubtless exaggerate in order to boost our score. And while most women would know what a question about "best friends" was getting at, many men might be far less sure: it is mainly girls who, from an early age, go in for designating a "best friend". Some of the books and articles that I have read make no distinction between "comradely" and potential or actual sexual – "courting" – friendships, some don't relate people's friendship patterns to the geography of where they live, or how long they have lived there, or whether their mother and sisters (or father and brothers) live nearby. Some don't take account of personality differences, which may govern not only our drive towards and our inhibitions about forming friendships, but also whether a man feels threatened if his wife has women friends in whom she confides, or a woman feels threatened if her husband has another woman as a friend. Although there is no doubt that in general woman suppress their emotions less than men do, and are more likely to confide in other people and themselves be confided in, there are wide differences among men and among women, as well as between them. There is, in short, no norm to which you should conform or feel you must judge yourself by.

PART TWO

The Ingredients of Friendship

4

Attraction

I like my friends, and they seem to like me. Over and above the other ingredients of our friendship – the acceptance, trust, and so on – there is some "chemistry", some force of attraction, that holds us together, and continues to do so even if we sometimes have disagreements, get on each other's nerves, or are temporarily preoccupied with our own lives. This attracting force is in part the *reason* why we're friends. Having first encountered each other at work or in some recreational or community activity, as time passed we discovered this mutual attraction – maybe it was there from the start and we were slow to recognize it, or maybe it actually grew and developed over a period – and chose to spend some time in each other's company and get to know each other. And our friendship just grew from there. As it did, and as our appreciation of each other and our pleasure in each other's company deepened, so the attraction between us grew stronger. All of my friends and I know many other people, and during our adult lives have come into contact with many more, and so have had lots of opportunities for striking up friendships. In some cases, of course, we have done so. But we have kept up our friendships with each other in particular because of the strength of the attraction that grew up between us.

For us, then, the process of becoming friends has involved mutual choice – choice prompted by this attraction. Not everybody gets the chance to choose their friends in this way. Or if they do, the field of choice may be very limited. People who live in an isolated village, or spend much of their lives within a minority community, or spend all their spare time in the company of work colleagues, may find themselves in this position. But they too may discover a mutual attraction to someone else within that limited range, especially if the other ingredients of friendship are present or develop between them.

What does this attracting force consist of? Where does it come from, what is its origin? Robin Skynner suggests that people are drawn to one another if they have similar or complementary family backgrounds. But what does family background give rise to? Sexual feelings? (A dating or courting couple tend to be similar to one another, just like friends.) Or maybe a yearning to re-create one or other of the relationships that was important to us in our childhood, perhaps one that ended abruptly or that gave us so much pain that, even as adults, we have not yet come to terms with it (the "unfinished business" syndrome)? Did our family background help to endow us with the confidence to do things on our own, or perhaps with a compulsion to "collect" people, as if we had learned from our parents that having numerous friends gave us status or security? Whichever is the case, the implication is that we can, in effect, be "conditioned" or "programmed" in our infancy or youth to associate certain kinds of feelings with a particular sort of person – with particular looks or mannerisms, or who behaves in a particular sort of way – and so to be attracted to them, or – conversely – to be put off by them.

On this line of argument, it is the child within each of us – embodying our psychological carry-overs from childhood – who is attracted to other people. If we're lucky, those psychological carry-overs are happy ones: we learned that some people had the ability to evoke good feelings in us and how to recognize such people and attract them to us. But if not, our child can get us into trouble – for example, when it is attracted to someone who promotes or resurrects in us uncomfortable and painful feelings, like the feeling of being unworthy. That's why we are sometimes unable to resist someone even though we can't understand what the attraction is, and know rationally that they are quite unsuitable, that we're being extremely silly and it's going to end in disaster. When people say "What on earth does she see in him?" (or he see in her), their mystification stems from the fact that they can observe only the grown person, not the child inside.

From my own experience and from observing other people, I am inclined to accept this argument. I do not, however, think that it can possibly be the whole story. I can see no inherent reason why our emotional development should stop at the end of childhood, and indeed there is plenty of evidence that for most of us it does not; for example, the experiences of having and bringing up children, sharing our own and others' grief over death, and co-operating with others at times of stress, all have a maturing effect on most of us. So grown-up people should be able to continue to develop their emotional apparatus to an adult level. What I mean by this is that (1) we confront and dispel the negative, painful psychological carry-overs from our childhood, so that they no longer distract us or inhibit us from making good relationships; (2) we keep hold of the positive, pleasurable psychological carry-overs from child-hood, and develop them and delight in them; and (3) we discover new ways – deeper, more perceptive, more mature – in which we can relate and react to other people. Thus we discover in ourselves a capacity to appreciate other people, to relish and enjoy their qualities – their spontaneity, perhaps, or the attention that they give to those around them – and especially the ingredients that they contribute to friendship. As adults we have more emotional resources than a child, and can thus be less egocentric: having had more experience, and given a modicum of imagination and flexibility, we will be better able to put ourselves in another person's shoes and see things from their point of view, and for that reason too be better able to appreciate them. And if we are emotionally adult we will also be much better at avoiding getting involved with someone unsuitable, even if the child inside us finds that person irresistible.

If we feel attracted to someone, it is highly likely that we're being attracted partly in an adult way and partly in a child-like one. How can we tell which? Adult feelings, I suggest, have a measure of confidence about them, as if we know very well that people do not fall out of friendship as they might out of love. Such feelings are not contingent from day to day on how the other person behaves; we don't have a sense of vulnerability, but rather the attraction is upheld by a sense of steadiness, durability, dependability. In contrast, child-like feelings are likely to have a compulsive quality – jealousy, possessiveness, and an inability to stop thinking about the other person, where there is a negative psychological carry-over; being gripped by excitement or exhilaration where there is a positive one. The child in us may very well have a sense of vulnerability about the enterprise. And if, despite the attraction that the other person holds for us, we are capable of being embarrassed by what he or she does; if we fear their anger, scorn, ridicule or indifference; if we fear that they might "betray" us – in all these cases we should recognize that our feelings are child-like rather than adult. Could it be, we should ask ourselves, that we learned in our childhood to have these negative feelings, and that we now find ourselves attracted to someone who has the ability to resurrect them in us?

No relationship between two people can ever be entirely free of negative child-like feelings, but some relationships – indeed, some friendships – will involve them much more than others. Sexual partnerships and family relationships, and very intense friendships too, will almost certainly bring negative child-like feelings to the surface at times, partly as a result of the psychological complexity of such relationships. But in general, in the friendships that I am writing about in this book the ingredient of attraction is based largely both on feelings that we learned to have as adults (appreciation, etc.) and on positive feelings that we first experienced as children and have managed to hold on to in adult life. In my view, then, the ideal friendship is a relationship between adults where there is mutual attraction based on both adult feelings and positive child-like ones.

To conclude this chapter, let me say something about my use of two words that we associate with attraction – "like" and "love". If two people are attracted to one another as adult to adult, without negative child-like feelings being involved, then I would say simply that they like one another. If the attraction is strong, then they may well also have a great deal of love for each other, by which I mean that they care for and about each other in a whole-hearted, generous, unstinting and undemanding way: they wish each other good for his or her own sake, not for their own. What I do not mean is that they love each other in the sense of "being in love", which, I fear, has more to do with compulsive behaviour than noble feelings.

5

Empathy and Rapport

What is empathy? The definition I like best is "the power of understanding and imaginatively entering into another person's feelings" (*Collins English Dictionary*). Dorothy Rowe, in *Depression: The Way Out Of Your Prison*, describes empathy similarly as "that special form of imagination ... which allows us to understand how another person experiences himself and his world." And Lillian Rubin, in *Intimate Strangers*, describes it as "the capacity ... for participating in another's inner life, for sensing another's emotional states almost as if they were her own."

We empathize – make use of our empathy – with many other people besides our friends. When we watch a play performed on the stage, or watch a film or TV play, we may find ourselves empathizing with one of the characters, experiencing their pleasures, their excitements, their dilemmas, their anxieties, as if they were our own. But the interaction in that situation is only one-way. By contrast, in day-to-day life, when we find ourselves empathizing with other people, they are often simultaneously empathizing with *us*. And what takes place is not only a sharing of each other's feelings: extra feelings are created, feelings of rapport between us. We get that "glow", that feeling of mutual warmth and "withness" – an echo, perhaps, of a positive feeling that we experienced in childhood.

This creation of rapport – sometimes in fleeting instants, sometimes sustained for hours when we're in the company of someone who is very close to us – is a daily occurrence in the lives of many people. Indeed, we see empathy at work all over the place. The motorist in the stream of traffic along the main road who catches the eye of another who is waiting to come out of a side turning, and slows to let him or her in, senses through empathy that bit of tension that they are feeling. Likewise the second motorist senses through empathy the desire of the first to have his or her little courtesy acknowledged, and gives a thank-you wave. Little warm glow all round. And when a woman in the queue at the supermarket check-out says to the woman behind her, "I really hate queuing" and gets the reply, "Especially when you've got to get on with all those other things when you get home", the chances are that through empathy each just *knows* what's in the other's mind.

To judge by the definitions quoted above, and by what I see of empathy at work, empathy has three components. One is the ability to pick up messages from another person. Not only spoken words but unspoken ones that require reading between the lines – oblique references, unfinished sentences, changing the subject – and also messages that are conveyed by tone of voice, facial expression, gestures and posture ("body language"), and "vibes". Partly this ability is an intellectual one – we use our eyes and ears and brain – and partly it is an emotional one – we *feel* what is going on. The second component of empathy is the ability, on picking up messages from the other person, to "reproduce" in oneself the feelings that they have. Again this might require conscious use of our brains, as when we make a positive effort to imagine what the other person is feeling, perhaps searching our memories to find a similar experience that *we* have had, or it might be an ability that comes naturally and unconsciously to us, without any effort or deliberation on our part. Whichever is the case, though, it does imply an ability actually to have feelings and to be aware of them. So even if we reproduce the other person's feelings unconsciously, we do admit them to our consciousness to some extent. The third component, which isn't evident in the definitions of "empathy" that I've quoted but is plainly essential to rapport, is the ability to "play back" these feelings, communicate them back to the other person – either by mirroring them or by responding to them in some other way – to show that we have reproduced them and see whether we have done so accurately. So if we're picking up "anxiety messages", we could respond either by becoming anxious ourselves, or by being appropriately reassuring.

Several writers have argued that empathy is something that women are well endowed with but men are not. It is a capacity "for which women are so justly known" (Lillian Rubin) and which men "lack" (Mary Ingham). The explanation of this difference is said to lie in the fact that boys, as part of the process of acquiring their "gender identity", repress their original identification with their mothers and the feelings of closeness that went with it. They resist anything that they experience as attachment – like mother's apron-strings – and fight against sharing feelings. Social pressures reinforce the suppression of feelings, and further inhibit the sharing of whatever feelings do find their way into a boy's consciousness. Girls, on the other hand, do not go through the same process in establishing their gender identity. While they do have a problem – that of separating from their mothers, which is made more difficult by virtue of having the same gender identity – this does not seem to lead to the suppression of feelings in the same way. Social pressures also push girls into being sensitive to other people's feelings, and help to accustom them to sharing feelings. As I argued in the chapter on "Who Are Our Friends?", boys learn to "affirm" themselves, girls learn to relate to other people. It should not be surprising, then, that women should have more empathy than men.

Undoubtedly there are some sweeping generalizations in all this. There are men who *are* well-endowed with empathy, just as there are women who aren't. To explain empathy or its absence in terms of a child's relationship with his or her mother is to ignore the relationship between child and father, to treat it as irrelevant, which strikes me as bad science as well as contrary to my own experience and that of others whom I know. But if we accept that in general women do have a higher level of empathy than men, does this mean that they score more highly on all three of the components of empathy that I described above, or on only one or two? It is significant, I think, that both Lillian Rubin and Mary Ingham base their conclusion that men lack empathy quite heavily on the fact that men talk much less about their feelings, and are relatively inarticulate where emotions are concerned. This certainly fits in with the theory outlined above, which suggests that men will suppress feelings and not share them. It follows that the second component of empathy – the ability to reproduce another person's feelings and admit them to our consciousness – would not be well developed. But as to the other two components, the evidence is much less clear-cut. As we shall see later on in this chapter, there is evidence that men do indeed empathize with each other, and do achieve rapport with each other, but in a way that involves doing things together rather than talking about their feelings. They do give out and receive messages, but they are conveyed between the lines of other messages that are to do with the job in hand, be it work or play. To overlook the vibes that men exchange with each other – and indeed that men and women exchange across the gender boundary – is to underestimate the empathy that men, or at least some of them, have.

People who possess the gift of empathy show it in a number of ways, and in their interaction with many other people besides their friends. They are alert to others, and give them their full attention when talking with them. Even when they're preoccupied with a job to be done, they show that they appreciate the companionship and colleagueship. When listening to someone else's story or problems, they respond not by exclaiming triumphantly "I know exactly how you feel!" – someone who does that is often wrong, I suspect – but by playing back the feeling (the third component of empathy), as if to check that they've picked it up correctly: "And then you don't know how to get out of it, do you", or "It's a bit like being ... isn't it." When talking to them you don't find it difficult to catch their eye – they don't gaze out of the window or over your shoulder – so you feel they're with you, and in touch. And when you say goodbye they watch you go, and synchronize their turning away with yours.

Very few people are completely lacking in empathy. People who behave in an unmistakably anti-social way – like those who want only to draw attention to themselves – are examples of this small category. But between that extreme and those who possess empathy in full measure, there is a wide range. It is difficult to place people on a spectrum, however: you may have empathy when you're with one group of people but not when you're with another, or there may be circumstances in which your normally good empathy deserts you. Nevertheless it is possible to draw a sketch of someone who is relatively lacking in empathy, by way of contrast to that already given of the relatively gifted person.

Someone who is relatively lacking in empathy when you are with them will not give you their full attention, and will often seem to be preoccupied with his or her own feelings. If you indicate to such a person that you're feeling unhappy or under stress, their reaction is likely to be "Never mind, dear", or even "Don't blame me", rather than to offer you a sympathetic ear. If a student presents a thirty-page essay to a teacher who lacks empathy, the reaction is likely to be a dismissive and angry "You can't expect me to mark more than five pages", rather than an interest in how the student became so "grabbed" by the subject. People like that teacher have little ability to gauge the effect of the messages that they consciously or unconsciously give you, so that when they try to be sympathetic, what comes out sounds condescending instead. Consequently they are quite often taken by surprise by how you respond to them. In conversation they may change the subject very abruptly and come out with things that are quite inappropriate. You may well get the feeling that what you are saying is not being taken seriously. If you leave their office or their home, they have switched you off and turned their attention to other things before you're out of the door. If you have ever tried to make friends with someone like this you probably know how intensely frustrating it can be.

To say that someone is lacking in empathy is not to say that they have no ability to form some kind of bond with other people. This bond may rely on shared history, as when they and an old school friend take it in turns to visit one another, or on a sexual relationship, or on doing things for one another, or on each providing an audience in front of which the other can perform. In all these kinds of bond, however, there is usually a very strong element of transaction: a major reason for doing something is that it will create on the part of the other person an obligation to respond. And a failure to respond may have the effect of torpedoing the whole relationship: have you ever heard anyone say, "I'm not phoning X; it's his/her turn to phone me", and not been struck by the amount of anger and resentment triggered off by the failure to comply with the assumed obligation?

Writers who have drawn attention to the subject of empathy have tended to concentrate on trying to explain the differences between men and women. This is perhaps what has led them to highlight psychological and social factors – the fact that only women mother, for example, and the different conventions about how boys and girls should behave. They have thus entirely neglected to look at what adults do to babies irrespective of their sex, at child-rearing practices. And strangely enough, there are books that discuss mother-daughter relationships in detail without making any mention of child-rearing practices. Yet the chances are that if you were born in Britain during the 1920s, '30s or '40s, especially into a middle-class household, you were brought up under a regime that could

49

hardly have done more violence to feelings of rapport and mutual warmth had it been designed for the purpose. This was the regime advocated by Frederick Truby King.

Truby King and his regime are portrayed by Christina Hardyment in her book *Dream Babies*. He was a New Zealander whose first involvement with the welfare of babies stemmed from his research among bucket-fed calves. Having reduced to zero their mortality from scouring (a disease resembling gastro-enteritis) by his "scientific system" of feeding, he turned his attention to human babies. His methods, which involved heavy reliance on breast feeding, were vigorously promoted and widely adopted. Before long infant mortality in New Zealand was halved. After the First World War his ideas were taken up in Britain, having by then developed into an all-embracing regime.

Truby King babies were fed four-hourly from birth, with few exceptions, and they had no night feeds. Quantities were laid down according to a rigid formula, and the importance of not over-feeding was stressed. Between feeds, they were left alone outdoors for long periods as much as possible. Their education, including potty training, began from the very first week. Parents were discouraged from hugging and playing closely with them for fear of transmitting germs. If they cried when they were left alone, that was simply giving their lungs essential exercise, and certainly not a reason to cuddle them or feed them, which would run counter to the aim of instilling discipline. How did Truby King babies feel? According to later critics, they (we) were hungry, thwarted, convinced of their essential unimportance, despairing of anything better, growing up self-controlled and emotionless. (These comments make no distinction between boys and girls, incidentally.) How did their mothers feel? Torn between the book and their maternal instincts, they felt distressed and guilty at the sound of continuous crying, and inadequate if the baby didn't develop according to the Truby King standard pattern. As for fathers, there was virtually no part for them to play at all when their children were only babies. (Of course, for many children born between 1925 and 1945 father was away on military service for part of their childhood, and mother fearful of receiving news of death or wounding, another fact that finds little recognition in the literature on the psychological make-up of the forty–sixty-year-olds of today.)

It is hard to see how being reared in this way could help a child to develop empathy (or indeed a firm sense of self). Self-control and lack of emotion imply an inability to admit one's feelings to one's consciousness, and so a fundamental requirement for the possession of empathy is missing. And if as a child one has learned to associate being thwarted and rejected with being dependent on someone and having close psychological ties with them; or to want desperately to be loved by people who are experienced as thwarting and rejecting, one is likely to encounter huge difficulties in relating closely to other people – especially if they have been brought up under the same regime. It may be, however, that the occasional moments when maternal instinct broke through and rapport was established between mother and child were so poignant as to leave an imprint out of all proportion to their frequency, or that the child developed an acute sensitivity to the "signals" given out by adults in his or her struggle to predict their behaviour and make sense of these terrifying, big people who did not respond to a baby's cries. A child who acquires that sensitivity would probably grow into an adult who possessed *one* of the components of empathy – i.e. the ability to pick up all sorts of messages from other people – but not the other important one, the ability to reproduce in oneself the feelings that are in the minds of those who send the messages. A Truby King baby, I guess, would be too preoccupied with his or her own frustration, anger and unmet needs, to absorb the mother's feelings, especially if those feelings *were* a confusing mixture of guilt and frustrated maternal feelings.

Is it possible for someone who did not learn empathy as a child to acquire it later in life? There is evidence that some parents – fathers as well as mothers – do indeed do so in the process of bringing up their own children. As one parent put it, "you grow yourself up at the same time" – by allowing the experience to reawaken the feelings that you had in your own babyhood and childhood, and then re-writing the script, as it were. Mothers seem to achieve this more with daughters, and fathers with sons. When I tucked my little son up in his cot, it was almost as if I was being tucked up myself. If we can make the imaginative leap and put ourselves in the position of that little person, struggling for autonomy and acceptance and recognition, there is perhaps some hope for us.

Of course, by no means all of us were reared on such a fierce regime as that of Truby King. It seems plausible that more intuitive or intentionally relaxed approaches to child-rearing would be likely to give a child more of an opportunity to acquire empathy, although how far this opportunity was utilized would presumably depend on other factors too. A more pertinent question so far as making friends is concerned is whether empathy can be taught to adults. One might expect that people who have undergone training as psychotherapists would have learned it, but books on psychotherapy say little about it and certainly don't offer instruction. Anthony Storr (in *The Art of Psychotherapy*) suggests that people who are attracted to the profession tend to be over-anxious to please and sensitive to what may be upsetting to others – perhaps because they had depressed mothers or particularly difficult, irritable fathers. So they already have one of the necessary components of empathy. But their sensitivity cannot be maintained without repressing considerable aggression, Storr says. If during their training they do not come to terms with the aggressive aspect of their personalities – and if you have had experience of "the games psychotherapists play" you may feel that some indeed don't – then they are certainly carrying with them an obstacle to empathizing with other people: they may pick up vibes but do not resonate to them because the aggressive feelings get in the way.

What are the lessons for the rest of us? Bearing in mind the three components of empathy that I identified earlier, we can try to improve our ability to pick up messages from other people – the first component – perhaps by getting into the habit of paying them closer attention when we're talking with them or doing something together. If we can achieve this, we'll probably get better at reproducing their feelings and playing messages back – the second and third components. But I suspect there are some obstacles to empathy, getting in the way of all three components, that we carry around with us, and that to make progress we need to learn to deal with these. Bottled-up aggression might be one such obstacle. If it led us to regard other people as competitors – automatically, without thinking about it – or got us into the habit of *judging* other people rather than accepting them as they are, it would certainly get in the way of empathizing with them. Preoccupation with our own concerns could, if taken to an extreme, be another obstacle – for example, if we're wholly absorbed in our work, so that we experience other people as distractions, or if we're always on the lookout for signs that other people are not treating us with the respect or deference that we think is due to us, or if we're so afraid of being disappointed that we pessimistically always look on the dark side of things, to protect ourselves, and so miss all the encouraging messages that other people beam towards us. To dismantle these obstacles it is necessary, I suggest, first to realize that they *are* obstacles, to want to remove them, and to choose to do so. Obstacles to empathy seem to constitute a prison, like depression, in that they come between us and other people, and to find a remedy we could probably do much worse than to follow the suggestions that Dorothy Rowe makes for finding a way out of "the prison of depression".

Before leaving the subjects of empathy and rapport, I want

to return to something that I mentioned earlier, that form of rapport that people – especially men – experience through *doing* things together, through shared activity and the conversation that goes with it. This shared activity and conversation have in themselves no emotional content whatever. The feelings remain unspoken, unarticulated, the empathy is mute, but the rapport is there nevertheless. John Berger, in his book *A Fortunate Man: The Story of a Country Doctor*, catches it beautifully: "The easiest – and sometimes the only possible – form of conversation is that which concerns or describes action: that is to say action considered as technique or as procedure. It is then not the experience of the speakers which is discussed but the nature of an entirely exterior mechanism or event – a motor-car engine, a football match, a draining system or the workings of some committee. Such subjects, which preclude anything directly personal, supply the content of most of the conversations being carried on by men ... in England today ... Yet there is warmth in such conversation and friendships can be made and sustained by it ... It is as though the speakers bend over the subject to examine it in precise detail until, bending over it, their heads touch. Their shared expertise becomes a symbol of shared experience. When friends recall another friend who is dead or absent, they recall how he always maintained that a front-wheel drive was safer: and in their memory this now acquires the value of an intimacy."

One conclusion that I draw from this story is that it is not valid to assume, as Lillian Rubin does when she discusses the differences between men and women, that being inarticulate where emotions are concerned is necessarily a sign of emotional impoverishment. Surely the men who are bending over the subject to examine it are empathizing with each other. It is not fanciful to see them as having, while they are together, a shared identity, the strength of which is – in the words of Phillida Salmon – "the strength of a personal story intimately shared, deeply reinforced". I wouldn't describe this as emotional

54

poverty. The bonds between men who do hard, skilled and dangerous manual work – miners, for example – seem to have the same kind of quality.

The passage from John Berger's book also highlights another very important point, I think. Imagine a meeting between two people, both of whom are highly empathic, with a high sensitivity to other people's emotions. If they are all sensitivity and nothing else, then both are like empty vessels waiting to be filled from the other: the consequence is that neither will be. Empathy they may have, but how can there be rapport in these circumstances? The excerpt from John Berger's book gives us the answer. You need a sense of your own self as well – which may be manifested in other ways, of course, than by a devotion to front-wheel drive – and actually to communicate that sense. Anthony Storr seems to be making this point when he writes: "Persons who are attracted to the practice of psychotherapy often seem to relate to others by identification with the other rather than by mutual self-affirmation on equal terms.... Some of their social encounters may consist of a monologue on the part of the person with whom they are talking, with the therapist making no more contributions than he would when a patient was freely associating. Although such a conversation may leave the other participant with a conviction that he has been talking to someone particularly 'nice', he may, on reflection, recall that the therapist has not said anything about himself, and that he therefore had had no real opportunity of judging whether he was nice or not." (Unfortunately Storr doesn't go on to ask what happens when two such psychotherapists meet.) The lesson is, I suggest, that in order to achieve rapport, to form and sustain real friendships, both mutual identification and mutual self-affirmation are required. On the one hand we need empathy, on the other we need a sense of our own self and the ability and self-confidence to reveal and affirm it. Certainly, if we reveal nothing of our own selves, we are sending out no messages (except that we are concealing ourselves), and if we are sending out no messages, no one can empathize with us. "Sense of self" is the subject of the next chapter.

6

Sense of Self

Imagine two people who feel an attraction towards each other
– a platonic attraction, no sex involved – and also find that they
easily empathize with each other. Does that mean that they
have everything that is necessary to make a real, close
friendship? I don't think so. Each of them also needs a firm
"sense of self", a sense of his or her own identity and
individuality, of who they are. In addition they must be able to
recognize the other person's identity and individuality, and be
prepared to respect them. To have a sense of one's own self
seems to be fundamental to making a good relationship of *any*
kind, but especially friendships. It is as if we each need to have
a firm "base" from which to reach out to the other person. And
it is as if our having such a base makes it easier for the other
person to recognize us – to see where we're at, so to speak – and
to reach out to us. Having our own firm base, we feel more
secure in ourselves, more confident of our identity and
individuality. We know ourselves, we know who we are. And if
our friends recognize and respect our identity and individuality, that has the effect of reinforcing and strengthening our
sense of self, so that it actually gains from the friendship.

Everyone who can give an informative answer to the
question "Who are you?" has at least *some* sense of self.
Whatever your reply, the very fact that you can give such an
answer shows that you have some concept of your own identity,
of who you are. "I'm a woman, my name is Mary, I'm a
pharmacist in a hospital." "My name's Peter, I'm eighteen, in
my last year at school." Even the barest description, so long as
it serves the purpose of distinguishing you from the mass of

people around you, demonstrates some sense of self on your part. You might, if you were answering the question, actually want to start with those features that most clearly distinguish you from everybody else: "I'm six foot six, half Russian, and a Buddhist." Or you might want to slip in a mention of your achievements: "I'm a schoolteacher, head of a department, female, thirty-three years old." "I'm an electrician, I've got my own business, I live with my wife and kids in Bromley." Perhaps you'd start with what seem to you to be the salient features of your life story: "I was born in London during the war ..." Or do you think of yourself first and foremost in terms of your relationship with other people? "I'm a wife and mother ..." Maybe you'd imagine trying to advertise yourself, stressing the qualities that you think you have and that other people would find attractive: "Bearded man, forty-four, passionate nature, sense of humour, non-smoker, seeks ..."

The notion of "sense of self" is quite a complicated one. It seems to have a number of different components, as is shown by the great variety of ways in which it is possible to answer the question "Who are you?" And all of these components, I suspect, have a bearing on our ability to form friendships. To try to make sense of them, and show how they relate to one another, I've made up a diagram, like a family tree, which is shown on the next page. This diagram isn't intended to demonstrate some stunning insight into the human personality, but simply to provide a helpful way of organizing a wide variety of observations about how people actually feel and behave. It works like this. First of all I'm saying that sense of self has two main components – *self-image* and *self-esteem*. Our self-image is literally what we see when we look at ourselves. So it comprises our perceptions of ourselves and is essentially descriptive – although hardly likely to be unbiased, given that we're not neutral observers of ourselves. Our self-esteem, on the other hand, is to do with the *judgements* that we make about ourselves. There are any number of "criteria" – scales – that we

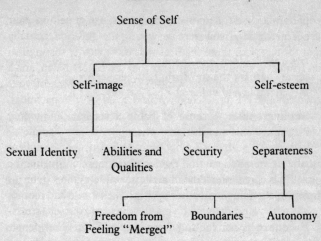

use for making those judgements: valuable/worthless, deserving/undeserving, strong/weak, important/unimportant, successful/a failure, to name but a few. Where we rate ourselves on these or other scales will reflect how we feel about ourselves, about the person behind our self-image.

Furthermore, it seems to me that self-image can itself be seen as made up of a number of components. These are perceptions of particular *aspects* of ourselves. There are perhaps four significant ones, which are shown in the diagram, in the third layer down from the top:

Sexual identity: A sense of confidence, whether high or low, in one's maleness or femaleness and particular sexual orientation (heterosexual, homosexual, or bisexual).

Perceived abilities and qualities: A sense of being able to do various things, of having physical, mental and social skills and capacities of various kinds, and of being a particular sort of person – generous, kind, independent, energetic, or whatever.

Security: A sense of feeling secure, or not; i.e. of being somewhere on the spectrum between secure and insecure, invulnerable and vulnerable.

Separateness: A sense of being a separate individual, distinguishable and distinct, or not.

Finally, it seems to me that the fourth of these – separateness – itself has three inter-related aspects, or facets, and these are shown in the fourth layer of the diagram:

Freedom from feeling "merged": A sense of being a person with one's own separate existence, rather than of being merged with someone else, overlapping with them or being joined to them (as if one had an emotional, as opposed to physical, Siamese twin) or even being a part of them: such a sense may be strong or weak, or indeed this freedom could conceivably be completely absent.

Boundaries: A sense of having one or more "domains" or territories that are more or less clearly marked out as one's own, with boundaries – sharp or fuzzy – around them. Such domains may be defined in terms of autonomy (see below), for example, or privacy, or knowledge which we have but others don't.

Autonomy: A sense of having, to a greater or lesser degree, the freedom to take decisions, such as decisions about our own behaviour and actions. The extent of this freedom defines an "area of autonomy", which may be thought of as one particular kind of domain, or aspect of our overall domain.

Put in a nutshell, my argument is this: we are more likely to have difficulty in forming and sustaining friendships if our self-esteem is low and if our self-image is elusive and unclear to us – if we are not confident about our sexual identity; if the picture that we have of our abilities and qualities is seriously out of line with reality or with the perceptions that a number of other people have of us; if we feel insecure and vulnerable, easily threatened; and if we feel we haven't established our separateness in all its aspects. But this needs to be argued rather than asserted, so in the remainder of this chapter I want to look in turn at each of these elements of sense of self, and examine how our ability to form and sustain friendships depends on having them, whether in large measure or small. I'll begin with the various elements of self-image.

Sexual identity

The difficulty that some men have in being friends with women seems to reflect a certain lack of confidence in their own sexual identity. These are the men who, as Nancy Chodorow puts it, "reject, devalue, and even ridicule women and things feminine". Mary Ingham, who interviewed nearly a hundred men in their mid-thirties, writes: "Some men who expressed patronizing attitudes about women described an ineffectual father, dominated by their mother, a father for whom they felt pity or contempt ... All of them claimed that they much preferred the company of other men." The explanation seems to be as follows. As they grow out of babyhood, boys – like girls – identify first with their mother. If a boy has a close personal relationship with his father, he learns a masculine role by identifying with his father and taking on something of his personality, behavioural traits, values and attitudes. But in the absence of such a relationship, he tends to identify with a cultural stereotype of the masculine role – big boys don't cry, men don't show their feelings – and also to associate masculinity with the negation of what he regards as feminine. (As we saw in the last chapter, boys seem in any case to repress their original identification with their mothers, as part of the process of acquiring their sexual identity.) Girls do not have the same problem, since no shift of identity is involved for them, although they do encounter others as they grow up, to do with their sense of separateness. This explanation clearly fits very well with Mary Ingham's observations. It is an explanation that takes no account of sexual orientation, however. It seems plausible that people who are uncertain whether they are heterosexual or homosexual might encounter difficulties in forming friendships, if it meant that the other person was forever in the dark about the potential scope of the relationship – as to whether it might develop into a sexual relationship or not, for example – and about what rules of behaviour – governing touching and so on – were appropriate. But I don't know of any studies that would support or disprove this supposition.

Perceived abilities and qualities

The problem that arises if our perception of our abilities and qualities is seriously out of line with reality or with the perceptions that other people have of us is that those people don't know whether to relate to us on the basis of our perception or theirs. It is as if we are an actor playing a part, and they don't know whether to relate to the actor or to the character that we are acting. Should they play our game and humour us, or not join in the game? The latter course may have the effect of making us angry with them, or even of devastating us if we are forced to confront the fact that we have been "living a lie". But humouring us will involve them in complying with our expectations of how we ought to be treated, and thus to some extent in living a lie themselves. We might of course be able to find and make friends with other people who are willing to share our self-deceptions and inhabit the same, more or less make-believe, world: for examples of this see fringe or not-so-fringe political or religious groups, or any organization that erects a barrier between itself and non-members who don't subscribe to its ethos and beliefs. But if, for instance, we expect other people to treat us as poor when we are in fact well off, or as well-informed and knowledgeable when we are not, or as compassionate when we are actually grossly insensitive to the suffering of others, our likelihood of making friends with normal people is about as great as that of finding a professional musician to accompany our singing if we are tone deaf and have no sense of rhythm.

Security

People who feel insecure and vulnerable are often very skilled at concealing the fact, even from themselves. They – we – may be able to give the appearance of being secure, especially if they acquire possessions, status, influence, qualifications, children. But these may only mask, and not remove, the underlying feelings of insecurity and vulnerability. And the mask will very rarely be complete: the feelings will still show now and then in the way that we behave. For example, if we tend to behave aggressively towards other people in certain circumstances; if we have a tendency to compare and judge and label other people, rather than accept them as they are; if we sometimes wall ourselves off from them and refuse to listen to them or expose ourselves to their emotions; if we are more liable than most to feel threatened and personally affronted by things that other people say or do (does it make you furious to think that other people might be talking about you behind your back?); and if we adopt a rigid and negative attitude to the possibility of new experiences ("I don't do X"), perhaps because we fear making fools of ourselves, then it may well be that buried somewhere inside us – and stemming, no doubt, from experiences way back in our childhood – are feelings of insecurity and vulnerability. Clearly these feelings, and the behaviour that they give rise to, will get in the way of forming and sustaining friendships. Any attraction that might be there is in danger of being swamped by the aggression; the wall that we erect gets in the way of communication; potential friends may well be put off if they feel that they are being judged rather than accepted. They may at first find the challenge to breach the wall an irresistible one, but the challenge may pall if penetrating one wall only reveals another. To make friends with someone who has a deep-rooted and fundamental sense of insecurity may be a long, slow, wearying process – and a person who is attracted by the challenge may not be someone who appreciates the contents of the bastion when they are finally, if ever, revealed.

Separateness

I suggested above that separateness, the sense of being a separate individual, distinctive, distinguishable from other people, itself has three aspects, or facets – freedom from feeling merged; boundaries; and autonomy. These concepts are inter-related: they are perhaps best thought of as different notions that various writers have used for making sense of the same phenomenon. Feeling merged means feeling that we are not someone with our own separate existence but instead overlap with or are joined to another person, or indeed are a part of them. That other person is usually someone with whom we have a close emotional tie. Thus Luise Eichenbaum and Susie Orbach (*Understanding Women*) write: "At times mother's sense of herself as a separate person dissolves and she experiences her daughter and herself as having the same feelings, thoughts and desires." They continue: "When this occurs it is hard for a mother to be appropriately responsive: she may be withdrawn at one moment and over-involved the next." Which illustrates how feeling merged may get in the way of making a good relationship. Daughters too may have this experience in relation to their mothers. Thus "the daughter's sense of self is fused with her sense of mother, so that in her attempts to separate from mother she may not know who she herself is. Trying to be her own person, she is nevertheless confused about where she begins and her mother ends."

It appears, then, that the state of feeling merged with their mother is one from which women emerge in the normal course of growing up. But according to Eichenbaum and Orbach, "many women never feel free of their mothers. They are not separate people, but experience mother as living inside, judging, binding, tempting and disappointing." The same writers also cite an example of a woman experiencing an unconscious merger with her (male) partner, one manifestation of which was that she felt acutely embarrassed in certain social situations by her partner's behaviour. Again the merger threatened the relationship, because the woman could deal with her feelings ("maintain her sense of control and boundaries") only by distancing herself from the relationship.

Sisters may have similar problems. Brigid McConville (*Sisters*) provides some interesting evidence about the compulsion that some sisters feel to define themselves in opposition to each other: "She's the artist, I'm the academic", and so on. She describes this as an elaborate system of "defence against merging", and gives examples of girls doing things purely for the sake of distinguishing themselves from their sisters, in order to establish their "different identity". Interestingly, only after this separateness has been established are they able to form close friendships with each other.

It is difficult to say with any precision what is the source, or sources, of the feeling of being merged. It appears that when we come into the world, as new-born babies, we have no idea that we are separate from mother, different beings. Gradually, in our first few months, we do get the message that she is physically separate from us, but in our early years we remain very much bound to her. We depend on her in particular to do many things for us, and to tell us what we can do for ourselves; we draw our very identity from her. And she in turn may regard her young child almost as an extension of herself. So in adults feelings of being merged may simply be "carry-overs", as it were, from periods when they were very young children or, more recently, themselves the parents of very young children. This seems to be more likely to happen to women than to men. "Just as the fact that there are no obvious differences between a girl and her mother makes the process of establishing a gender identity easier for girls than for boys, the problem of separating – of defining and experiencing self as an autonomous, bounded individual – is harder" (Lillian Rubin). Perhaps, then, women have a greater tendency to feel merged in any close relationship that they enter into as adults. How is it, though, that a woman can feel merged with her sister? Is it to do with shared experience at the most impressionable time of one's life, or with being children of the same mother? Or is it to do with the social environment, the attitudes and behaviour of other people? It is difficult to answer this question because there may be more than one process going on. Siblings – brothers as well as sisters – are liable to get *labelled* by their parents and other people. "Why can't you be clever like your sister?", a boy might be asked by his teacher. Or one sister might be labelled "the dutiful one", and the other "the pretty, flirty one" by their parents. So they might be reacting against these labels and the expectations that go along with them as well as against feeling merged. The process of establishing separate domains of expertise – the clever one, the practical one; the artist, the academic – would be a positive way of reacting to both at once. At any rate, it does seem safe to conclude from the circumstantial evidence that feelings of being merged may be so strong that they make it difficult for the person experiencing them to have a friendly relationship with the other. These feelings thus require to be shed – partially if not completely, some of the time if not all of it – and replaced by a sense of separateness if the two people involved are to become friends.

Some illustrations may make this clearer. Take the case where we or our would-be friend, or both of us, start off feeling merged with one another – if we are parent and child, for example. If the parent, say, experiences the child as an extension of himself or herself, by virtue of that fact they won't be according the child autonomy, nor will they perceive the child as having a domain of his or her own. (I shall discuss the concepts of "autonomy" and "domain" in a moment.) They won't, in other words, be accepting of the child's own sense of self. Consequently it is unlikely to occur to the parent to offer the child an equal share in deciding what they should do together, or to take seriously views that the child expresses that are different from his or her own. If the child feels merged – or submerged! – he or she will find it difficult to imagine existing independently of their parent: hence the young child in a playground who stops playing every now and again and runs back to Mummy or Daddy to check that they're still there, or the older child suddenly overcome with panic at having to do some task on his or her own when in the past they've always had parental help with it. The child is also likely to be easily embarrassed by things that his or her parent does, as witness the notorious capacity of schoolchildren to be embarrassed by their parents' behaviour in front of their friends.

Now, all this might not matter so much if it applied only to parent/child and child/parent relationships. It would get in the way only of those parents and children becoming friends with each other. But it seems that when we form close relationships with other people, a certain amount of "transference" may take place, with the other person becoming something of a mother-figure or father-figure for us. (Do *you* get embarrassed by things that your spouse or partner does?) Not only may men be attracted to and marry women who resemble their mothers, and women be attracted to and marry men who resemble their fathers: the same kind of forces may underlie the attraction that we feel towards people whom we would simply like to be friends with. So there is the danger that we will develop a sense of feeling merged with people whom we become friends with, particularly if our childhood experience has left us with a propensity or tendency to want to merge with someone else. It may also be the case that if we have a sense of feeling merged with our spouse or one of our parents, we are carrying them around with us, so to speak, with the consequence that we react to events or situations or people as if we *were* them. (Eric Berne, in *Games People Play*, makes the point that all of us are capable of switching from one personality state to another, behaving sometimes like an adult, sometimes like one of our own parents, sometimes like the little child that we once were.) One possible result of this is that when we are with someone else – such as a friend or someone we'd like to be friends with – we might have feelings of guilt if it's someone whom our spouse would distrust or resent, or we might find ourselves judging them in the way that our parent would. In this situation, our ability to accept and respect the other person, and to relate to them honestly and openly when we are together, is bound to be considerably impaired.

On now to the subject of boundaries and the domains that they define. We can, I think, distinguish at least three different kinds of domain, within which we have respectively autonomy, privacy, and special knowledge. Think about the demands that children make as they grow up – for freedom to decide and do things for themselves (autonomy), not to have to expose their bodies and their thoughts to other people (privacy), for it to be recognized that they know better than their parents what goes on at school or in their friends' homes (knowledge). What is of interest here is whether the boundaries of our domains are visibly clear and sharp, or fuzzy – unclear and ill-defined – and also whether this matters to us. Is it important to us that our boundaries *should* be clear and sharp? So far as autonomy is concerned, many human beings – in our society at least – seem to have a strong drive to establish and defend a domain for themselves. If you work in a big organization, it may be quite important to you and your colleagues to know where your respective responsibilities and powers begin and end. And if someone trespasses on someone else's "patch", the owner of the patch may be quite disconcerted and upset; even someone who is normally equable may become flustered and angry. This drive may be stronger in men, reflecting their generally greater competitiveness, but it is certainly not confined to males. A similar drive to establish and defend a domain seems to operate where both privacy and knowledge are concerned, as witness the claims of doctors, lawyers and other professionals that they have monopolies of expert knowledge and should not be accountable to lay people in matters of judgement or professional conduct.

What is the source of this drive to establish and defend a domain with clear and sharp boundaries? Insecurity always seems to have a lot to do with it. It is always the most easily threatened and least confident people who are the most conscious of their status, and the most fearful of having their territory encroached on, and who, when their judgement is challenged by a lay person, defend it by labelling it "professional", rather than by exposing their reasoning to public view. Similarly it may be that young children who are habitually naughty (on their parents' definition) behave in that fashion not out of sheer perversity but out of insecurity, whether through lack of attention or through receiving ambiguous and inconsistent messages from their parents about what they may and may not do: behaving naughtily is a way of provoking the parents into reacting in a very unambiguous way – physically unpleasant, maybe, but psychologically very reassuring, in that it is absolutely clear to them, at least for the moment, where they stand and where the boundaries of tolerable behaviour are.

Some people reach adulthood with only a hazy idea of where their boundaries are vis-à-vis other members of their family. Conceivably this in itself could be a cause of insecurity. They have not had the experience of distancing themselves from their parents, siblings and others, and of finding clear mutual boundaries through establishing their separate identities and a stable balance of power between them. So they have fuzzy boundaries, a condition which would seem to be a natural accompaniment to a tendency to feel merged with someone else. It would follow that this condition too would be a greater hazard for women, and for the same reason, that the problem of defining and experiencing oneself as an "autonomous, bounded individual" is harder.

If you are a person with fuzzy boundaries, relating to other people presents problems. Your fuzzy boundaries may lead you to behave in any of a variety of ways, ranging from the highly aggressive to the highly defensive. At the aggressive end of the spectrum, not only will you have no clear idea of where your own boundaries are, you will almost certainly be no respecter of other people's boundaries – because you are unable to see where they are. They will experience you as intrusive – perhaps you make use of their territory and possessions as if they were your own – and interfering: if you feel that you know better than they what they ought to do, it will not occur to you to respect their boundaries and keep your advice and urging to yourself. Clearly this could scarcely be conducive to forming and sustaining friendships with them. If you can actually sense that the other person does have clear boundaries, even though you can't locate them with any precision, you may find that a very attractive feature in them – to the point, indeed, of wanting to adopt their boundaries as your own. If your eventual aim is matrimony, you would probably be saying "All I want is to be close to you". The other person, however, may be very strongly motivated to defend his or her autonomy. If they are unsure about their own boundaries, they may feel very threatened by your approach, even though initially they may have found it flattering. And once the two of you are trapped together in the relationship, there can only be difficulties ahead, with the obligation-creating techniques (see below) that you learned as a child, and that you use to get inside the other person's boundaries, likely to grate increasingly on your partner and arouse his or her defensiveness more and more, possibly to the point where they back out of the relationship altogether. (Divorce, of course, is a method of establishing a boundary, although someone who has been divorced may find it very difficult not to think of herself or himself as half of a couple, which is sure to create boundary problems when they try to relate to other people.) It may be that aggressive "macho" behaviour too is a method by which people with fuzzy boundaries try to find clear ones, giving the appearance of invading and colonizing as they try to find boundaries by pushing up against other people's, and seeing how far – using economic, physical or emotional means, singly or in combination – they can take over their territory. But whatever form the aggressive behaviour takes, it can hardly be conducive to forming and sustaining even a friendship, much less a partnership.

At the defensive end of the spectrum, if you are somebody with fuzzy boundaries you may adopt the technique of retreating, of abandoning any claim to autonomy beyond the very limited area that you can feel confident about. In effect, you retract your boundaries until they enclose your citadel or fortress. Potential friends will recognize, sooner or later, that there is a bit of you that you will not allow them to reach, and this will inevitably constitute an obstacle to the growth of friendship. Even if you are married, or in any other sort of stable relationship, you will declare this citadel a no-go area to your partner. Should he or she come across it, and try to explore it, you will instantly freeze and deliver a rebuff. Here lies a bit of your precious autonomy and privacy, and it is your prerogative to defend them; indeed, you are strongly motivated to do so. All that your partner can do is to retreat to a citadel of his or her own. If you tacitly agree to respect each other's no-go areas, you might well be able to attain some sort of equilibrium, and lead a stable and "civilized" life together – or what passes for "together" – especially if there are some areas of your lives, such as work or shared leisure activities, where you are both self-confident and clear about your respective boundaries.

Evidently, then, having fuzzy boundaries can, like having a tendency to feel merged with someone else, seriously inhibit our ability to form and sustain friendships with other people. This would be particularly likely if we are insecure as well. How far does that ability depend on the third aspect of separateness, autonomy? Why should a lack of autonomy, or equally a failure to appreciate how much autonomy we do in fact have, make it difficult for us to form and sustain friendships?

As I said earlier, when we come into the world, as new-born babies, we are almost entirely dependent on others – mother in particular – for our well-being. As we grow up, we want to do more and more things for ourselves: the drive for autonomy comes into play. And as we successfully extend our repertoire of activities, so our autonomy extends, and correspondingly the boundaries of our "autonomy domain" push out further and further. Frequently this brings us into open conflict with our parents: as our boundaries push out, so theirs are pushed back. So the boundary is a mutual one: it represents the "frontier" between them and us. But parents also begin – perhaps quite early – to use more subtle weapons. Instead of "Thou shalt not do X", the message is "You don't want to disappoint your loving parents by doing X, do you?" In other words, instead of defining our boundary by issuing prohibitions, they inhibit us by putting us under obligations. We *could* do X, it still lies within our boundaries, but the consequences of doing it are likely to be unpleasant: we are liable to feel guilty that we have disappointed our parents, let them down. (Religion too may be employed to induce feelings of guilt.) If we are frequently on the receiving end of such treatment, it may affect our whole attitude to taking decisions. In particular, it may again result in insecurity on our part, in timidity and lack of confidence: we probably don't do things that we otherwise would do because we fear the consequences or are simply uncertain what they would be, or we feel that we have to ask whether it's OK to do this or that. Thus, along with this lack of confidence may go a heightened sensitivity to other people, not only our parents: we are always looking to others to discover what their expectations of us are, seeking for cues as to how we should behave. Girls especially seem to be socialized into acquiring this heightened sensitivity. We may also become "allergic" to this technique that is being used to control us, which may breed in us an anger and resentment at what feels like manipulative and underhand treatment. We may carry over this allergy with us into adulthood, so that when somebody else employs such a technique, or we imagine that they do, we react with a fear or fury that is much more to do with our own history than with the other person's actual behaviour.

One consequence of having been conditioned in this way is that we may be inhibited from forming friendships because we fear the obligations that they might bring – fear, perhaps, that we won't be able to handle them, that we might find ourselves vulnerable again. We are afraid to "jeopardize our autonomy", as Jill Brown puts it, afraid to take on the giving-and-receiving element of friendship in particular, if our history leads us to associate giving and receiving with obligations. Fear of obligations and lack of confidence in our own autonomy seem to be two sides of the same coin. Whichever side is uppermost in our minds, our ability to form and sustain friendships will be impaired.

So far in this chapter I have been talking about ways in

which elusiveness or lack of confidence or lack of clarity in the various elements of our self-image can affect our ability to become friends with someone. Let me now go on to ask how that ability is affected by our self-esteem, the judgements that we make about ourselves as to whether we are valuable or worthless, deserving or undeserving, and so on.

There have been a number of studies by psychologists of how low or high self-esteem affects our ability and drive to form friendships. They are reviewed in Steve Duck's book, *Friends, For Life*. "People who have frequently experienced rejection in the past, and who blame themselves for it" – this is where the self-judgement comes in – "are likely to maintain low drives towards friendship through fears of further humiliation. They will be likely to remain socially unadventurous, reserved and cautious, will feel vulnerable in new relationships ... They often express the deepest cynicism and doubts about other people's motives in relating to them, and are constantly on the watch for signs that the other person is insincere, or is entering a relationship with them for instrumental reasons, like a desire for sex." Again, experience in childhood, as well as subsequently, is influential in producing these feelings and behaviour. People with high self-esteem and people with low self-esteem react very differently in social encounters. Steve Duck gives an example. Imagine that you are talking to someone at a party, who goes off to get another drink. If you have high self-esteem you are likely to assume that the other person is thirsty, but if you have low self-esteem you might very well assume that he or she was bored by your conversation. Research also shows that children who meet with rejection respond in different ways. A child with high self-esteem will tend to bounce back and try again, whereas a child with low self-esteem will tend to withdraw, make fewer and fewer attempts to initiate other friendships, and so become isolated. Some of the latter, however, suppress their perception of being rejected and instead, say the psychologists, turn into

74

"incompetent attention-seekers" – noisy, rebellious, boastful, and ultimately a nuisance to teachers and classmates. It would be interesting to see such studies set in their social context, with the consequences of factors such as differences in social class being explored.

What, if anything, can we do to gain a firmer sense of self – a clearer and more distinct self-image, a greater degree of self-esteem? To answer this question would take a book in its own right – or rather, since there can probably be no single answer that is exactly right for everyone, an infinite number of books. But we can get help in this from our friends, as we shall see in Part Three, and from the above discussion we can also get some idea of the basic "tools" that we need to tackle this task.

First of all, a good level of self-awareness is absolutely crucial. Without this we simply cannot know who we are: we are likely to be confused about our abilities and qualities, possibly about our sexual identity as well, and to feel insecure, because we actually don't know who the person is that inhabits our body. If we are to achieve this level of self-awareness, we must be prepared to look honestly at ourselves, to question things that in the past we have taken for granted, and to view ourselves through the eyes of others – not necessarily to accept what they say, but to consider with an open mind the possibility that their view of us, where it differs from our own, might be more realistic and accurate. Opening ourselves up in this way, exposing ourselves, requires some degree of self-confidence, and so we need to develop this as well. Fundamental here is the ability to live with ourselves, to accept that we are who we are – even if we don't wish to continue to be that person, and decide that we are going to change. Living with ourselves also implies accepting that what happened to us in the past did happen and can't be altered, although we may learn to view it differently, as when we come to see that a rejection by someone whom we loved was not only a painful and traumatic event but also one that led us to become a more emotionally aware person, with a greater sensitivity to other people's emotions.

Another requirement is to be aware of how we interact with other people. We need to be aware of the obligation-creating games both that we play on them and that they play on us. This is particularly important if our sense of separateness is weak, if we have problems with feeling merged, boundaries, and autonomy. (For instance, if someone says to you, "Why were you behaving so strangely?" you need not accept the obligation to justify yourself to them, and especially not to accept unquestioningly that description of your behaviour.) If we can see what games we're vulnerable to, and get some idea of how and why they make us uncomfortable or produce distress in us, we're well on the way to learning how to cope with them and thus to eliminating or at least reducing our vulnerability.

The issue of separateness poses a distinctive set of problems, which are liable to be different for men and women. Boys, after being forced at an early age to accept their separateness from their mother as part of the process of learning their different sexual identity, go on to positively affirm their separateness. This is subsequently reinforced by social expectations. Men tend to identify with a concept of independence, as Lillian Rubin found (although it didn't seem to correspond very well with reality), and not to require prompting to assert their autonomy, associated as it often is with "attractive" images of power and authority. But the territory-consciousness of many men, their insistence on having well-defined and well-defended boundaries, suggests that behind this assertiveness there lies insecurity. The boundary walls hide this insecurity from other people's view, but – as we saw in the last chapter – they also act as great obstacles to empathizing with them, thus getting in the way of relating. Not only are men inhibited from learning to relate in childhood, but it isn't easy for them to learn to do so when they are adults, although they may be better at it than their reticence about emotions may suggest. For men, then, how to cope with insecurity may be the underlying problem when it comes to relaxing barriers. Women, on the other hand, may in childhood have learned all too well how to relate. Growing up accustomed to merging, they may later not find it easy to establish a worthwhile and meaningful domain of autonomy or to respect other people's. Those who find themselves economically dependent on a man for years on end may come to feel a strong sense of insecurity, which acts as an obstacle to empathy for them too.

There are two other tools that are essential if we are to strengthen our sense of self. One is a willingness to experiment – to be flexible and to learn. This does mean being prepared to take risks, to expose ourselves. Occasionally, perhaps, we *will* look silly, or get a rebuff: an occupational hazard of sticking your neck out is that you sometimes get your head chopped off, metaphorically speaking. But as we find that we can take risks and survive, that the sky does not fall in on us, our security and self-confidence will improve out of all recognition. The other tool that we need is resolve, the *determination* to take risks, to do something for ourselves. Fortunately we all have the capacity to summon up resolve when it's really needed and we can see what we have to do.

There are several books available offering practical advice for anyone who feels that they need to do something about aspects of their self-image and self-esteem. Anne Dickson's guide to developing one's assertiveness, *A Woman In Your Own Right*, is first-rate, and the techniques that she describes can be equally useful to men who need them. Marsha Linehan and Kelly Egan's *Asserting Yourself* is another good book on the same lines. Much of the advice contained in Dorothy Rowe's book, *Depression: The Way Out Of Your Prison*, is relevant to anyone with a blurred self-image and low self-esteem, not only people recognizably suffering from depression. She is particularly good on the subject of coping with fears and coming to terms with one's vulnerability. Her view of depression as a prison is especially helpful, because her suggestions are couched in terms of how to dissolve barriers or find a way through them or around them. Muriel Schiffman's book, *Self Therapy*, a handbook of techniques for personal growth, is another clearly written and well-illustrated practical guide. What these books have in common is that they can help us to understand how our past gets in the way of our present and future, and then to learn how to prevent it from doing so. They can help us to realize that sense of self is not manufactured, it is discovered. To discover it may take a journey of exploration, of experiment, of trial and error, but, as Krishnamurti put it, what we will find is that "There is nowhere to go. You are already there." It was inside you all the time.

Reading this chapter may have prompted you to look at yourself and evaluate what you see. Maybe you've been pleased with what you have found. But maybe, like many other people before you, you've found this kind of self-examination and self-questioning difficult to do. It's not a comfortable kind of exercise to undertake, and if – again like others before you – you come to the conclusion that you haven't got much to show for your twenty or thirty or forty or fifty years or whatever, it can be a rather saddening experience. If that's so in your case, just remember this. To do this sort of evaluation without pulling any punches with yourself, without deluding yourself, requires an enormous amount of courage and an enormous amount of honesty too. If you've discovered those two things within you, you can credit yourself with two supremely valuable and important qualities, which will stand you in good stead in everything you choose to do with the rest of your life. What's more, everyone else who values those qualities will value your friendship too. There are much worse situations to be in!

In this chapter I have argued that having a firm sense of self – a clear and distinct self-image, high self-esteem – is essential to being able to form and sustain friendships. But the interaction is a two-way one: the friends that we have support our sense of self, our friendships strengthen and reinforce our self-image and self-esteem. That two-way interaction is really what the rest of this book is all about.

7

Acceptance and Respect

In the chapter on "What Is Friendship?", I suggested that one of the ingredients of friendship is that friends accept and respect each other. I want to say something here about what this means, about what it feels like to be accepted and respected by someone else, and to accept and respect them.

Being accepted and respected by someone implies a number of things – being welcomed, invited into his or her company; being taken into their confidence; being treated as an equal, as someone of the same status; but in particular it means being allowed to be oneself. To be allowed to be oneself implies just that: we are not required to change the way we look, or the clothes we wear, or the opinions we hold, or the way we speak, as a condition of being allowed to be someone's friend. Indeed, if someone "allows" us to be their friend it is not the same thing at all as allowing us to be ourself, and what you have is not a real friendship as I understand it, because it is a one-way, one-sided relationship, and not a two-way, mutual one. Being accepted and respected, then, means that once we are someone's friend new conditions are not forever being imposed on us, we are not continuously being judged and evaluated to see whether we are still good enough to be their friend: the friendship, and thus the status of "friend", is something that we can take for granted. By the same token, if we are someone's friend we need never fear that something we say or do will suddenly and without explanation lead to them rejecting us and ending the relationship.

The feeling of being accepted and respected makes a major contribution, I suspect, to that warm – sometimes almost melting – glow that we can feel when we're with a friend. And it carries with it a feeling of being safe, of being able to drop the defences that we put up in normal, day-to-day life. It may be that people who experience it find it so satisfying because it reminds them of pleasurable feelings of that kind that they experienced when they were very young, as babies in their mother's arms – the "carry-over" phenomenon again. And it may be that those who don't experience it as adults fail to do so because they did *not* experience it in their infancy. For them, being accepted by someone else, being allowed to be close to another person, may be rather disconcerting, possibly raising in their unconscious all sorts of warning signs of the "people whom you are close to may suddenly turn round and hurt you" variety. They may find being accepted wonderful at one moment and impossible the next, being unable to trust that the wonderful bit is real and won't suddenly vanish. This is wholly consistent with one of the messages of the last three chapters, that our ability to be part of a friendship depends on our personality and personal characteristics. To develop that ability will require us to think about who we are, and about how we might change.

To accept and respect someone else implies a number of things that are the counterpart of being accepted and respected. Thus it implies that we welcome the other person, and invite them into our company; that we take them into our confidence; that we treat him or her as an equal, as someone of the same status; and in particular that we allow them to be themselves, with all that that entails in terms of not requiring them to change their looks or clothes or opinions or anything else in order to fit in with our conceptions and preconceptions of what is "right" and "proper". One obvious thing that follows from this is that we find some people much easier to accept and respect than others. There will inevitably be some people whose looks or clothes or opinions are so alien to our own that there is no point in trying to accommodate ourselves to them.

There will also be some people whose characteristics are so close to our own that to accept them requires no accommodation on our part at all. But there may well be others who share some of our own characteristics, so we do have some things in common with them, but not others. If we want to have them as our friends we must learn not to be judgemental towards them, not to expect them to conform to our standards, and not to feel free to criticize them – to shoot from the mouth – when they don't so conform.

It would be easy for me to advise you to treat others as you would wish them to treat you, from which it would follow that if you wish them to accept you, then you must accept them. The trouble with this advice is that it may actually be extraordinarily difficult to accept someone else. For example, we may find ourselves feeling that their adherence to different standards implies a rejection of ours: even if we don't experience this consciously we may feel it deep down. Or we may feel vaguely threatened by it without quite knowing why. Perhaps you are a parent who wants to be friends with your child, yet find yourself wholly unable to stop yourself from feeling that you have a right to criticize your child and expect him or her to adopt your standards and conform to your expectations. Such difficulties in accepting another person may stem from all sorts of personality traits, past experience and things that we take for granted: perhaps the "confrontation" awakens feelings of anxiety and insecurity which are only dimly perceived and are hard to talk about, let alone explain. It may be easier to blame these painful feelings on the other person rather than look at ourselves and analyse what's going on inside us, but – as is usually the case – while it is easier to blame than to analyse, it is also much less fruitful and constructive. I am sure that if we repeatedly encounter difficulty in accepting other people, that is a clear sign that we need to examine ourselves. Such analysis may help us to discover the source of these painful feelings; alternatively, it might show us that we are consistently selecting as "targets" for our friendship people who are simply not appropriate, and then help us to understand why. At all events, the thing to bear in mind is that the people who are most successful in accepting others are those who have acquired a degree of self-awareness, who have come to terms with, who have learned to accept and respect, themselves.

8

The Obligations of Friendship

The bond between friends is provided not only by the feelings that they have for one another stemming from their mutual attraction, but also from the feelings of obligation that each has towards the other. Loyalty is a good example. If you are someone's friend, you would probably feel obliged not to tell other people things that they had told you in confidence, or things that they themselves would clearly not tell others. You would probably also feel obliged not to criticize them in public. Research has shown that these are virtually universal rules of friendship (Michael Argyle and Monika Henderson, *The Anatomy of Relationships*). Obligations, then, impinge on our autonomy, our freedom to do what we like. The fact that they exist in our own minds, that we *feel* obliged, makes them no less potent, for we know that if we disregard them and behave as though they didn't exist, we would soon have no friends left. Sometimes friends do want to translate a general obligation to be loyal into a specific commitment: "If I tell you, will you promise not to tell anyone else?" Similarly, two friends going to a dance might agree that neither will go off with someone else and leave the other on his or her own.

Obligations allow us to make assumptions and have expectations about the future. If your friend comes to you tomorrow and asks for help with something, you will probably feel that you ought to give it if you can, even at the cost of some inconvenience or sacrifice to yourself. And you would expect the same of him or her. Part of being friends is that you can count on one another, is it not? You have a stock of goodwill for one another, and you *expect* that it will continue to be available, especially if it has been for some time, growing as your friendship has grown. And you both know that people rarely "end" friendships in the way that they end sexual relationships, "affairs". History itself creates expectations. If you and I have spent the last five Christmases together, I may expect that we will do the same next Christmas. My expectation may be perceived by you as creating an obligation for you. If you envisage doing something else next Christmas, you may feel that you will be disappointing me, that you will be responsible for my disappointment. If you are reluctant to incur this responsibility, you will feel that your freedom to do something else is fettered. That's obligation!

Here is another little scenario. Imagine that your friend says to you: "I want to see you again very soon. Promise you'll phone me?" There's a certain pressure to say "yes". After all, you don't want to hurt his or her feelings, and you don't want to end your current meeting on a sour note. But afterwards you might well feel vaguely resentful at having had this promise "extracted" from you. Observe the technique that has been employed against you. Your friend has placed on *you* an obligation, a responsibility for not hurting their feelings, instead of taking on him- or herself the responsibility for coping with the sadness or whatever that could result if you don't in fact phone. Unfortunately for the person who extracts the promise, the technique is actually counter-productive, and not only because of the resentment that it produces in you. One way for you to respond is indeed to point this out. You can say: "I want to *choose* to ring you. That way you will know that when I do phone it's because I really want to. If I phone only because I've promised to it won't be worth having, it won't signify that I care about you, so you'll probably want more evidence, and more again, that I do." The fact of the matter is that the solution to one's insecurity cannot be found in extracting promises from someone else, for there can never be enough of those: it can only be found within oneself.

You will find that with practice it becomes quite easy to identify the manipulative techniques that other people use on you: recognition is half-way towards mastery. And you can try to adopt Robin Skynner's rule for family therapists, which can be applied in any situation where you have no reason not to feel reasonably at home: establish clear boundaries for yourself by saying what you are, and are not, prepared to do, and avoid being manipulated into changing those decisions – although you should be ready to listen to reasoned argument – "while being very friendly and encouraging through it all". Note the need for resolve as well as boundaries, and the importance of being firm, but also gentle.

Expectations may be created not only via obligations but also through psychological mechanisms coming into play. You may come to represent to your friend one or even more key figures from his or her past or present, and they, albeit unconsciously, direct towards you the feelings and attitudes that they have towards that figure (the transference phenomenon that I mentioned earlier). Clearly, if you are being regarded as a father-figure or a mother-figure, you are being expected to behave in a certain way, and pressure may be put on you, an attempt made to create obligations, to get you to behave in that way. Transference is perhaps more common among sexual partners – "men marry their mothers, women marry their fathers" – than it is among friends. And in general there are fewer and weaker ties of obligation between friends than there are between family members, not only because the relationship is less complex psychologically but because there is much less dependence of one on another for economic support, domestic care, or social status.

Let me pursue the comparison with families a little further. One of the things that families do is to provide us with a bit of "social structure". We know where we belong, where we fit into the society in which we live. The existence of obligations between us and other members of our families plays a large part in giving us that satisfying feeling, and the existence of obligations between us and our friends serves a similar purpose. In relation to our friends, *we know where we stand*. And they likewise know where they stand in relation to us. Both our friends and we ourselves know with some degree of confidence what place we occupy in each other's lives, indeed, what compartments we occupy. Moreover, not only do we know where we stand in the here and now: our knowledge gives us both a degree of confidence, as I noted above, that our respective places will not suddenly change. In other words, we project our perceptions of each other into the future: we form mutual expectations of each other, and these expectations are "synchronized". Let me use some examples to explain what I mean.

If you are friends with someone, the places that you occupy, the places that you assign to one another, may be defined in many different ways. For example, each of you may be the other's "best friend", meaning by that that you tell each other the most intimate details of your respective domestic lives, and that you both feel a closeness to the other that is not matched by any other relationship that either of you has. Or perhaps you and a friend are both members of a badminton club: you yourself go every week whereas she can't manage it so frequently, but you have an understanding that when she does turn up you will partner each other in doubles matches. Or maybe you and your friend are lovers: you have separate homes but take it in turns to sleep at each other's place. These three relationships, as described in these terms, are all established, "steady state", ongoing ones, which implies not only that they have a past – i.e. they have reached this state and continued in it over a period of time – but also that they have a future – there is an expectation on both sides that they will continue, for the time being at least. Thus the two of you have mutual, synchronized expectations of each other. You know where you stand.

The things that, as friends, you do and feel together, serve to reaffirm your respective "commitments" to the relationship. They provide each of you with evidence that the friendship is still alive and can be depended upon. It is this continued reassurance that provides the basis for the expectations you have, that allows you to feel that you can safely *depend* on each other.

That we can confidently hold such expectations is of crucial importance in our dealings with our friends. Imagine what it would be like if, every time you rang up your best friend, you had to open the conversation by asking, "Am I still your best friend?" Not only would you feel inhibited from confiding in your friend; your evident lack of confidence in the durability of his or her feelings might well give rise to doubts on their part.

That we know where we stand in relation to people who are our friends should not be taken to mean that such relationships are necessarily ossified. Circumstances change, and so do people. The balance and nature and depth of a friendship may change with the passage of years: indeed, if it didn't one would suspect that it had been reduced to nothing more than a collection of rituals. But some friendships may be more fragile, less robust, less able to accommodate themselves to changes. Or rather, the friends may lack, singly or collectively, the skills and motivation required to maintain the friendship. I shall talk about stress between friends in a later chapter.

Perhaps "knowing where you stand" in relation to someone sounds to you awfully like taking them for granted, and you may not be too happy about this. My answer would be that in any friendship there must be things that are taken for granted, on both sides, but that this is emphatically not the same as *presuming* on the other person's goodwill – taking something for granted without any indication from the other that you have their agreement to do so. In any sustained friendship there will be a continued flow of indications from both sides about what it is OK to take for granted, with both people being sensitive to and "reading" accurately the indications that the other gives. To presume – which, like me, you may find wholly obnoxious – is to overstep the mark, to ignore those indications.

Finally, it is necessary to stress the subjective element in all this. You may think you are a particular person's friend – but are you really? How do you know? One of the saddest pieces of information that I have come across in reading about friendship (in Michael Argyle's book) is the finding of a survey carried out in Toronto in the 1970s, that only thirty-six per cent of friendship choices were reciprocated, i.e. Jim may have said that Fred was his friend, but there was only a one-in-three chance that Fred said the same of Jim. If there is a disparity, with the lack of mutuality of obligations that it implies, the two of them can hardly be said to be friends on any of the criteria that I have been advocating. If Jim thinks he knows where he stands with regard to Fred, but has in fact got it wrong, it suggests that there is not a great deal of rapport between them, for example. Perhaps we should all ask ourselves whether people whom we think of as our friends actually do think the same about us. It might be a painful exercise, but if it leads to greater honesty and less self-delusion, perhaps we might thereby lay down firmer foundations on which to build our friendships in the future.

9

Caring and Cherishing

Friends are people whom we care about and cherish, which means that we feel an involvement with them, an involvement which is part and parcel of our relationship. To say that we care about and cherish them is to describe the importance that they have for us, the place that they occupy in our hearts and minds. To feel this involvement is an essential ingredient of "nurturing" – another dimension of it, as it were. To give time to someone and allow them to confide in you – which many writers seem to equate with nurturing – without feeling this involvement, without really caring and cherishing, is to make the relationship between you a hollow mockery of friendship.

We show that we care about and cherish our friends not only by taking part with them in the "interactions" that I describe in this book – doing things together, talking and confiding, giving and receiving, etc. – but in the way in which we take part, in our "style", in how we behave. That we care about and cherish our friends is associated with having certain feelings towards them – we warm to them, we feel loyal to them, we have love and affection for them – and when we have those feelings our style and behaviour carry and radiate them. They show in the way that we look at our friends, talk with them and touch them. We find ourselves making little acknowledgements, giving reassurances, exchanging hugs and cuddles, having spontaneous little chats about minor events of the day as well as discussing big issues and problems, remembering birthdays and other anniversaries, asking after each other in a way that automatically shows that we've been thinking of each other even when we're apart, being relaxed and confortable but quietly alert to each other when we're together, being attentive in a way that shows that we take each other seriously and not patronizingly. For you and your friend to pay little attentions (plural!) to each other, consistently, is one of the biggest things that you can do to sustain your friendship. Among other things, it will provide a foundation for your self-esteem and resilience. For example, if you and your friend demonstrably care about and cherish each other, you will find that you are able to let yourself be laughed at and taken down a peg sometimes, without feeling that you or the friendship are threatened.

What is it that prompts and enables us to care about and cherish another person? Clearly we must be able to experience the feeling of warming to another, and to recognize it in another person when they warm to us. And we must possess the emotional "machinery" for spontaneously translating that feeling and recognition into the involvement that caring and cherishing imply. Are the propensity and capacity to care and cherish fixed in us, then, by the time that we become adults – whether at a high, low or intermediate level – or can we acquire them? Are they latent in us, could they emerge if we allowed them to? These questions are much easier to ask than to answer. What I would suggest, though, is that if we want to discover our potential for caring and cherishing it is necessary to allow another person's vulnerability to impinge on us, to get through to us – as happens when we hold our new-born baby in our arms – and to peel off the layers of self-absorption and preoccupation with our own concerns that get in the way of involving ourselves with someone else.

What does it feel like to know – to have some evidence – that you are cared about and cherished by a friend? If you are aware of what feelings you have, and can put words to them, you would perhaps say that you matter to your friend, that you are important to him or her, that you feel you aren't alone, that there's someone else "there", even if they aren't physically by your side. And because your friend *chooses* to care about you and cherish you – their feelings are not associated with responsibility, as may be those that a parent has for a child – that they do so reflects a judgement of you, an evaluation. Evidently you are worth caring about and cherishing. Hence the boost to your self-esteem that you feel.

Many of us crave to know that we are cared about and cherished. No doubt this craving, like so many other elements of our personality, has its roots in childhood experiences. Deep down, it may be that we all have this craving, but while some of us are consciously aware of it, others are not: this could reflect the fact that it is actually, but unobtrusively, being fulfilled (for a husband by his wife, for example), or that it is being repressed, perhaps because we have a fear of being dependent on other people or because we fear deep down that there is no prospect of it ever being fulfilled. It may be that these fears are the greatest obstacle to our being able to care about and cherish others.

10

Trust

Most of us would probably agree that trust is an essential ingredient in any close relationship. However, people use the word "trust" in different ways, they mean different things by it, so if we are to find out what the particular significance of "trust" is, we must first examine these various meanings.

One context in which we talk of trust is that of one person confiding in another. For example, psychotherapists talk of patients having enough "trust" in them to be able to confide in them, by which they evidently mean that the patient feels a sense of assurance that the therapist will neither divulge what has been said, nor disparage or laugh at the patient and thereby diminish his or her self-esteem. Second, we "trust" someone when we believe what they say about their motives and intentions, even if there is a lack of supporting evidence, i.e. to trust them (or have trust in them) is to accept their assurance that they really will do what they have said they will. Third, we use the word in the sense of trusting someone's judgement, i.e. of feeling assured that if we follow the course of action that they recommend, or if we allow them to do whatever they think appropriate, the consequences will be better for us than if we don't. When we talk of trusting someone with our life, it is in this sense that we are using the word. Fourth, we "trust" someone when we believe that they won't desert us even when they find out things about us that they don't already know, e.g. "what sort of person I am underneath".

These different usages of the word "trust" have two notions in common. One is the notion of assurance, or confidence, about some situation or state of affairs *in the future*. And the other is the notion of taking a risk and thereby putting something at stake. To feel that you can trust someone is to feel that you can safely risk the consequences of telling them something or depending on their judgement or goodwill, a statement with which, I would guess, few people would disagree. But note that it is quite meaningless, it signifies nothing at all, unless we specify what is at stake, what we are trusting the other person with. If we risk the consequences of disclosing our most secret anxieties, what is at stake is the possibility that we will be regarded as ridiculous or bad, or both: our very self-esteem and our relationship with at least one other person may seem to us to be in jeopardy. By contrast, if we risk the consequences of disclosing nothing more than a fear that someone at work who is junior to us is going to be promoted over our head because of favouritism, a fear that it would be reasonable for anyone in our position to have, we are hardly laying our self-esteem on the line at all. In the same way, you could trust someone with your life or you could trust them with nothing more than a loaf of bread: so to say that you trust someone, without saying what you would trust them with, is to say virtually nothing. (The smart and technically correct answer, by the way, to anyone who says to you, "Do you trust me?", is "It depends on (a) what the stake is, and (b) what the risk of losing it is: can you tell me what circumstances you have in mind?" This answer may not, however, satisfy the questioner.)

Trust, then, grows along three "dimensions". The more you trust someone, the more you will be prepared to put at stake, whether in terms of your psychological or social or material well-being; the greater the confidence you will have that the risk of losing it is low; and the wider the range of circumstances will be in which these two conditions apply. And to say that a particular person is your friend is to imply that you would stake quite a lot, and be pretty confident of not losing it, although you might perhaps want to qualify your description by referring to the circumstances of your friendship (for example, "My friend at work", "the friend I play badminton with", or "my best, most tried and trusted friend").

The build-up of trust between two people who become friends will take place on all three dimensions, although it will automatically reach a limit on the third if the friendship is restricted to a particular sphere, such as work or a leisure activity. It will also, of necessity, take place over a period of time, since confidence about taking risks can be gained only through experience, as can knowledge about how someone else behaves in a variety of circumstances. Moreover, because finding out how far you can trust someone is by its very nature a process of observing and, in a sense, testing, it needs to be handled with quite a lot of sensitivity and so cannot be rushed. It also calls for rapport, because this isn't a process of cold, logical, computerized calculation that I'm talking about, although my references to "weighing risks" may give that impression: gaining confidence in someone else involves divining in them a steadiness, soundness, or a *dependable* reservoir of commonsense, joy, magic or whatever … whatever, indeed, your desires are.

Rapport will also help you to understand – to comprehend sympathetically – the *limits* to trust, the point beyond which it is not reasonable to expect your friend to put you first, for example. We all lead our lives under a variety of social obligations (to members of our families, to other friends, etc.), and under a variety of social pressures (to support charities, to play a part in local activities). In any particular situation, your friend may well have to resolve a conflict between, on the one hand, his or her obligation and spontaneous desire to do something for your benefit, and, on the other, obligations and pressures that militate *against* doing that thing, whatever it is. Rapport between you will enable you to put yourself in their position, to imagine what it is like to experience their dilemma, and thus to limit your expectations and to say to your friend,

"It's all right, I understand". Even if it is after the event, when your trust in your friend has been damaged by something that he or she has done, rapport combined with a bit of knowledge can help you to explain what happened and thereby limit the damage – or even eradicate it and perhaps deepen the friendship. Dorothy Rowe gives an example: "A mother may be horrified to discover that her son is stealing money from her purse and spending it on sweets. What she does not know is that he feels that he has to purchase his popularity at school and he does not trust her enough to tell her." I am sure that, for at least some mothers, the horror at a son's untrustworthiness would, on finding out the reason for his behaviour, be immediately overtaken by deeper feelings of sympathy and a desire to help him.

To talk, as I have, of trust as inevitably involving risk is to underline the fact that everything we do in this world – indeed, our very existence – is attended by uncertainty. It is helpful, I think, to make a distinction between two different kinds or sources of uncertainty. On the one hand, there is uncertainty about how people whom you know personally are going to behave, about how they will respond (to you, perhaps) in some future possible situation, about what they will do next week or month or year. On the other hand, there is uncertainty about what fate has in store for you, about how your life could be affected by economic or political changes, say. It is natural for human beings to seek to reduce the uncertainty in their lives, to some extent at least: it is important to the great majority of us to have security of tenure of the home that we live in, for example. Where we can't buy certainty, though, how should or can we respond to uncertainty? One thing that you might try to do is to remove the uncertainty from your life, as far as possible. You could try to adopt a self-sufficient life-style, cutting yourself off from the economic systems of production, distribution and exchange that bind the rest of us together. And you could cut yourself off from other people by not placing any trust in them, so that there is no possibility of them letting you down or surprising you by behaving unpredictably. The problem here is that even if you can isolate yourself from the rest of mankind economically you cannot do it emotionally without, it seems, severely disabling yourself: as Dorothy Rowe points out, to adopt an attitude of all-round distrust to the world is symptomatic of people who are very depressed.

If we cannot eliminate uncertainty from our lives, or pretend that it doesn't exist, how can we deal with it? The alternative technique is to build some sort of cushion into your life, by developing friendships which will enable you and your friends to give each other mutual support when unforeseen things happen. You don't know what will happen in the future, but you and your friends do know that you can count on each other's support when whatever it is does happen. This of course implies that you trust one another, and in particular it implies that you accept that uncertainty, that residual uncertainty that can't wholly be eliminated, that remains in each of you, because you are human beings, and also different people, under different obligations and pressures. While you may choose your friends for their dependability, and bestow your trust upon them, you cannot bind them to behave in ways that are predictable to you: you must accept their prerogative of uncertainty. And if it should happen that your trust is, to your mind, abused, let yourself learn from the experience, and on the basis of your greater understanding of your friend – and theirs of you – forge a new, deeper, and stronger friendship. Certainly the experience is unlikely to be more destructive of your friendship than is the refusal to accept uncertainty as a fact of life and forever looking to commitments from your friends to reassure you about the future. The search for certainty about the future is not only inevitably doomed to fail: it will damage, if not destroy, your ability to live in and enjoy the present.

11

Giving and Receiving

One of the central features of friendship is that friends give to one another, and thus receive from one another as well. They give help in all sorts of practical ways – such as sanding floors, making curtains, minding the children – and in the form of emotional support – comfort, reassurance, encouragement. They give of their time and their attention and, where emotional support is concerned, their nervous energy and "spirit". If you are familiar with the experience of being drained after a lengthy session of comforting and reassuring, you will know very well that raising someone else's spirits is not achieved without some cost to you. One of the good things about friendship, though, is the way in which – in the normal course of events, at non-crisis times – friends reinforce each other's spirits. Friendship is energizing. It actually increases your capacity to give.

A crucial aspect of giving to our friends is that we do so freely, without a quid pro quo – something in return, by way of compensation or reward – being sought or offered. It is in this generosity that we can see the "loving" nature of friendship. Over a long period – months, perhaps, or even years – there is probably a balance, in so far as these things can be measured, in each direction. It is important, however, that each individual instance of giving is not seen by either person as part of a transaction, and it is important for two reasons. First, because if the gift is seen by the giver as part of a transaction, as putting the recipient in his or her debt, it is highly unlikely to be spontaneous: the implication is that the giver has first made a mental calculation of what he or she might expect in return, or is making such a calculation at the very moment of making the gift. And second, from the recipient's point of view, knowing that something is expected in return will almost certainly detract from the quality of the gift and its value: comfort with a price on it is likely to be experienced as not very comforting at all.

A friend, then, is someone with whom you have a stock of credit, as they do with you. So you can feel free to ask one another for help. But no one's stock of credit with another person is unlimited. Genuine friends have sufficient rapport with you to recognize where these limits are. They won't "dump" their anger and aggression on you, to the extent that you are left frazzled and depressed while they walk away whistling cheerfully, relieved of their burden.

Giving and receiving take place of course not only between friends but between people in various kinds of unequal relationship, such as parents and children, senior and junior work colleagues, teachers and students, blood donors and anonymous recipients. Such relationships may contain within themselves some of the qualities of friendship, but mutuality is absent or constrained by virtue of the inequality that is built into the situation. The disparity of status and resources makes it very difficult, if not impossible, for the gifts in each direction ever to balance out.

There is something extraordinarily important about giving. It is actually a very great privilege to be able to give. One of the demoralizing effects of poverty is that it denies you that privilege. "One must be poor to know the luxury of giving!" (George Eliot, *Middlemarch*). To feel warm towards someone but be denied the opportunity or the means to give them anything, to make any tangible demonstration of your warmth, can be a most bitterly frustrating experience. It is surely one of the joys of looking after a very young child that there are no limits to your freedom to bestow on him or her your loving care. By the same token, one of the great pleasures of friendship is that it allows you that magnificent form of self-expression, the making of a spontaneous gift. And in the making of that gift, the recipient – your friend – plays a crucial part, not only in receiving your gift but in doing so in a way that is truly accepting – that is to say, not attempting to make it into one side of a transaction or appear to be an act of condescending charity.

It follows from all this that part of being a friend to someone is that you are able and happy to take the role of recipient of gifts from time to time, conferring on your friend the privilege of making a gift. If you are not able and happy to take this role, you should ask yourself whether you really are their friend, and whether they really are yours. Is there something that prevents both of you from accepting a gift from the other without feeling obliged to make immediate return or give humble thanks for their being so kind? It is true that some people do have difficulty with giving and receiving, irrespective of who the other person is. Possible reasons for this might include resentment at being expected to give – at Christmas, for example – or fear that the gift will be rejected by the recipient as inappropriate or inadequate; or a feeling that you are unworthy of a gift and must therefore repay it immediately. Such resentments, fears and other "negative" feelings seem to reflect a poorly developed sense of self.

12

Talking and Listening

We all feel impelled to talk to other people. This is not just in order to get through day-to-day life but because, it seems, this feeling is built into us: simply by virtue of being human beings, we have an urge, a drive, to communicate. Most of us, I think, feel distressed if we are ever cooped up on our own for days at a time. If you have a telephone, you probably get quite angry if it goes out of order, and do your utmost to get the service restored as soon as possible. And if you are elderly and living on your own, you probably like to do a little bit of shopping every day – if possible at "proper" shops rather than supermarkets – for the sake of the chance to chat with whoever you bump into in the shops or in the street.

Even little exchanges have value for us. Remarks about the weather may be nothing more than ritual, but even they give us some "pay-off" in that they serve to reaffirm our status as members of the human race, and we would probably feel quite snubbed and hurt if neighbours and shopkeepers stopped exchanging such little remarks with us. Such rituals may be the first step in forming a friendship, as when people go on to ask each other "How are you?" and after a while actually find themselves telling the other person how they are, instead of giving a ritual response such as "Fine, thank you".

Talking is a medium for conveying all kinds of messages. We use it to give news, to describe what has been happening to us and how we feel about it. We use it to make jokes. We use it to demonstrate our values and attitudes, approval and disapproval, and to try to persuade others to adopt our point of view. We use it to try to bring pressure to bear on other people, to make them feel under an obligation to us and thus to do what we want them to. We also use the medium of talking to ask for or offer help, to express sympathy and give advice. But talking is rarely a one-way activity, except where someone is making a speech or giving a lecture. Usually, and especially where friends are concerned, it is a matter of taking it in turns to talk, and while one talks, the other listens.

What is involved in listening? A friend who is a good listener hears not only the words that are spoken and the metaphors used, but the tone of voice and its pitch and inflections, and hears whether the words come tumbling out or are measured out in orderly fashion. This listener will hear the silences as well as the words. He or she will also register how the talker sits or stands and gestures or fidgets. Thus this listener will pick up umpteen messages, unconscious as well as conscious, and – knowing the talker already – will detect whether something is different from usual. A good listener will also make appropriate sounds and gestures – murmurs and nods and looks – that encourage the talker, and show that he or she has their listener's attention.

A worthwhile conversation between two people engages them. It enlivens, entertains, exhilarates. A good, satisfying discussion will be energizing intellectually, as when you find yourselves sparking ideas off each other. It is important that you should both have an appropriate conversational style, of course. To use a tennis analogy, what is called for are long rallies rather than the smashing of each player's services out of court. For example, if you open a conversation by saying, "My teenage son said to me ..." and it meets with the dismissive reply "Just like a teenager", that's the end of the conversation, and you have to start again if you want to get a dialogue going.

But conversation involves not only talking and listening. We *think* while we're talking and listening and in the pauses in between. Although much conversation is to do with small things in life – "What's the best way to Cambridge from here?"

– and is often, especially among men, more to do with scoring points off one another – "I did it in twenty-three minutes once: you really do need four-wheel drive, six cylinders and a turbocharger on these cross-country runs" – not all of it is. It is in meaningful conversations with our friends that part of our personal development takes place, as we form, try out and put together bits of our "view of the world" – what we take for granted about how the world works, what can be changed and what can't, what's human nature, and what the proper place in the world is of men, women and children. We learn from and with our friends. I suspect that this joint learning process plays a major part in forging between friends that emotional bond which I have called "rapport".

Talking is also a medium for *confiding* in someone else, disclosing our selves. Again, this seems to fulfil a basic human need, and as I argued in the chapter on "Do We 'Need' Friends?", it appears that self-disclosure is actually essential to our mental health. When we want to confide in somone, what sort of person do we look for? Someone who can be trusted not to divulge our confidences, and indeed not to exploit the vulnerability that we reveal. (If, say, we show another person what things make us feel guilty, we are presenting them with a weapon that they could use against us if they were so minded. So we want to have some assurance that they will not be so minded.) We also want someone who shares our view of the world and can appreciate our feelings: we want to have some rapport with them. Someone who will give us their time and attention and some reassurance, and show that they do want to receive our confidences. And someone whom we can rely on to accept us, or continue to accept us: this implies that they won't express disapproval of our thoughts or behaviour, or be embarrassed by what we tell them or the way in which we tell it, especially if in disclosing our feelings we lose our self-control, as when we break down and cry. Our confidant(e) must also be someone who in turn we won't be embarrassed to confide in.

Some of these requirements could certainly lead us to choose a friend to confide in, rather than perhaps a trained professional counsellor or psychotherapist. If you already know your friend as someone whom you can trust, with whom you have rapport, who will give to you and accept you, the choice may be instinctive and obvious. The question of embarrassment, however, may be more problematic. If what you want to talk about involves your sexuality or an extra-marital liaison or something that you are ashamed of, and it's a subject that you have never talked about before, you might judge correctly that to your friend it is something of a "taboo" subject, and that he or she would indeed be embarrassed if you raised it. Or if you want to talk about any aspect of the relationship between you and your spouse, and your friend is a friend of both of you, your loyalty to your spouse could make it embarrassing for you to confide in that particular friend. So if you did confide in them, you would keep some details to yourself, and some at least of the benefits that you hope for from confiding would be lost. In that case, if you have no other friend to turn to, you would perhaps be better advised to seek help from someone with training and experience in counselling.

What exactly do we do when we confide in someone, and how do we benefit? One thing that we do, of course, is to "get things off our chest". If you have been kicking yourself for something you have done but wish you hadn't, or haven't done and now it's too late but you wish you had, simply telling someone else about it may make you feel much better. If you are angry with someone, talking about your angry feelings to another person often defuses them, and you become calm. Talking about them to the person you are angry with may have the same effect, and not necessarily after a row. William Blake captured it:

I was angry with my friend
I told my wrath, my wrath did end.
William Blake, *Ms Notebooks*

But there seems to be more to confiding than merely recounting events and expressing feelings. When we confide, we are telling our story, and it is a story which we ourselves have written, in our heads if not on paper. In writing it we "make sense" of what has happened to us, we give it meaning. As Phillida Salmon puts it, in her book *Living in Time*: "As the authors of our personal story, it is we who must select, from the myriad happenings we witness daily, what belongs to the story and what lies outside. Only we can weave what we select into the narrative, only we ourselves can link what is happening now with what has passed, and what may yet happen in our lives." And in telling our story to someone else, we are not only making it known to them, we are *committing ourselves* to it – repressing doubts and uncertainties, imbuing it with concreteness. That is why when we confide in someone we do require an audience but we don't require much from them beyond signs that we have their attention and interest.

Confidants do not always get the choice of whether they want that role or not. (They should, I think.) As a confidant you may find yourself embarrassed for a number of reasons by what you are told. You may have been socialized by your upbringing into not talking about certain matters, such as sex. Or your friend may reveal such naïveté that you actually find it impossible to get on the same wavelength, and can see no tactful way of pointing this out. Or you may fear that your friend may later regret the outpouring, and this fear may grow with every detail that is revealed, until you are literally squirming with embarrassment. Or, if it is the case that you are also a friend of your friend's partner, you may find it extraordinarily distressing to learn of problems between them: the information that you are being given may make it impossible for you to relate to the partner on the same terms as previously. In this situation, you may feel – and you may be right – that an attempt is being made to enlist you as an ally against the partner. While it is undoubtedly a privilege to be admitted to another person's innermost thoughts, it is not a privilege to be grasped at greedily. On the contrary, you may want to make it clear that there are limits to what you can "take on board", and that if these limits are overstepped you will feel that your goodwill is being trespassed upon.

Finally, there is a lot of evidence that women confide – especially in each other – a great deal more than men do. Even among young children it has been observed that girls disclose personal details to each other much more than boys do (Phillip Hodson, *Men*). This seems to result from having both a greater "drive" to confide and fewer inhibitions about confiding, as well as a greater readiness to be confided in: there is evidence that in some married couples husbands "tune out" when their wives try to exchange confidences and discuss feelings with them. Behind these differences there seem to lie the same factors that I have discussed in earlier chapters, to do with the different psychological development of boys and girls in infancy and their subsequent socialization, with girls being taught to relate and boys to conceal their emotions.

13

Doing Things Together

One of the most visible features of many friendships is that the two friends "do things together". They may visit each other's homes, give each other a hand with work on the house or in the garden, play badminton or darts, make or listen to music, go shopping or to art galleries or football matches, or share in a hobby of some kind. Observe what they are doing. They are not only sharing an experience, they are experiencing each other. Each reveals facets of his or her personality; the other becomes aware of these, both consciously and unconsciously (without registering them), and responds, again both at conscious and unconscious levels. If you watch a man and woman dancing together for the first time, you will see a process of mutual adjustment taking place, as they get used to each other: if you ask them afterwards how they did it they will be able to describe some of it – "I had to take bigger steps than usual" – but it will be very clear that physical technique forms only a small part of the interaction. Certainly the exhilaration that both feel when they find themselves in harmony is due to a good deal more than just technique.

When you do things together with someone else, especially if you talk to each other at the same time, you experience them more fully and more spontaneously than if you do nothing more than talk. In tackling a concrete task, in co-operating, in reacting to events, they (like you) reveal their inner qualities in an unrehearsed way. So you learn about them and absorb what you learn: their qualities and their "style" rub off on you, so to speak. It is as if, in a way, you become one person: a dancing couple who fit together is a very apt example of this. It may be that the satisfaction that we get from this experience, the physical rapport that we feel, has its origins in our earliest infancy, when we felt what it was like to be wholly at one with our mother. At all events, it is quite clear that the pay-off we get from doing things together extends well beyond the satisfaction of a job completed or a game won or made enjoyable.

In doing things with someone else, then, we not only learn but we absorb and develop; we become in some respects a different person from what we would otherwise be. We also have the opportunity, if we want it, of learning about ourselves, of seeing ourselves as others see us. By seeing how our friends react to us, we may discover aspects of ourselves that we want to change. For example, if our friends are sometimes very wary of us, it may be because they have seen in us a capacity for anger which we manage to keep hidden from ourselves by repressing it. Or our friends may react with delight when we show a side of ourselves that we are normally diffident about revealing, and so we feel encouraged to allow it to develop and blossom. If we have a number of friendships, of course, we can play different roles in them, show different sides of our personalities, and accordingly develop in different directions.

To be in the habit of doing things together with a friend is to have a relationship that has continued in existence for a period of time. The time dimension is important for two reasons. The history of shared experience provides a bond between you. You are linked together through the shared memories – "Do you remember the time when ...?" – and through your shared development, the "rubbing off" of each of you on the other. And the past continuity provides you with a basis for having expectations about the future – not necessarily that you will continue your present activities for ever and ever indefinitely, but sufficient to enable each of you to look forward to what you do together, to enjoy planning for it, and to savour it in advance. And when you actually do it, when it makes the transition from a thing of the future to a thing of the present,

what you are doing is "reaffirming" your friendship, reminding you of – and renewing – your commitment to it.

It is of course true that friends do not continue doing the
same things together for ever and ever. Our interests develop
and change, we move on to different stages in our "life cycle",
our physical and other capacities and our financial resources
change, we may move house away from one another. But the
fact that we have a history of doing things together gives us a
basis for continuing to relate to each other as friends – for
continuing to care about and cherish each other, for example –
even though we no longer do those things together.

It is not only the sharing of activities that is important for us
and our friendships. What is also important is the way that
those activities are managed and organized. For some of us,
those activities are intermingled and jumbled up with others
and with social life in general, so our friends play a number of
different roles in our lives, or even – if our lives and those of our
friends are closely intertwined – constitute a kind of extended
family. For others, however, activities with friends seem to take
place more often in self-contained "compartments" in our
lives. We meet, "do our thing" together, then part and return
to the mainstream of our respective lives. In keeping our
friendships in compartments in this way, we are acknowledg-
ing that our friends and ourselves exist within a social context,
which may contain numerous links of obligation – especially to
do with family and economic activities, such as earning a living
– that bind us to other people. These compartments slot in to
the rest of our lives in a way that is relatively simple, in that
there are few if any cross-connections: what goes on in the rest
of our lives will have only a limited effect on what goes on in
these friendships, and vice versa. Such a harmonious detach-
ment is not always achieved, however. Spillover and conflict
may occur – when friendship and family obligations start to
compete for your time, or if, say, your partner feels excluded by
the friendship and begins to intrude upon it. But in general,

because compartments are (by definition) visibly marked out and reinforced by custom – "Friday night is club night" – they are both more easily defended and less threatening than they otherwise would be. For this reason they tend to be a socially acceptable way of organizing friendships within our lives.

Within the friendship, the fact that it occupies a compartment in the life of each of you, and that you recognize this, imparts a measure of stability and also control to the situation. From your point of view, it helps you to resist any pressure that might be forthcoming from your friend to extend the amount of time and other resources that you give to the friendship. The existence of boundaries that are defined in terms of time helps you to define boundaries in other ways too: it helps you to "ration" your participation in the friendship, to control, if you wish, the extent to which you reveal yourself, or allow access to other parts of your life. Probably one of the conditions for a successful friendship is that the two of you should be in agreement about the rules for rationing what you contribute; you need to have an understanding, even if you don't – as you probably won't – actually talk about the rules that you're going by.

Friendships that are contained within compartments may have a special value in that they provide us with controlled opportunities – and it is we who are in control – to experiment, to try out different roles and "personas". To the extent that while we are occupying one of these compartments in our lives we are insulated from day-to-day pressures and from the scrutiny of family, workmates, etc., we have a degree of freedom – depending, admittedly, on what our friend is like – to adopt a different style, to behave in ways that we would not normally, to talk about subjects that are taboo at home and work or with other friends, and to see how it feels. (This is of course what young people do, but I see no reason why the freedom to do it should be restricted to them alone.) Moreover, if we have problems in general in defining our personal boundaries – the boundaries to our personal autonomy, our scope for decision-making – and in defending them against encroachment by our partners and others, our compartments, once we have established them, provide us with very visible boundaries. Their very visibility makes them, when necessary, easier to defend than "fuzzy" boundaries, and so we can get some practice in acquiring this valuable skill.

PART THREE

Making and Keeping Friends

14

Some Basic Principles

The purpose of this chapter is to draw together some basic principles that could guide us in our approach to making friends with other people. First is the principle that before we can make friends with other people we need to be friends with ourselves.

By being friends with ourselves I mean quite literally that we should feel towards and treat ourselves as we would our friends. Using the chapter headings of Part Two as a checklist, we can see that that would imply a number of things. First, that we should accept and respect ourselves, which means having a firm sense of self – a clear and distinct self-image, a high level of self-esteem. Second, that we should certainly value ourselves sufficiently to feel some obligation towards ourselves – a responsibility for looking after our bodies and our minds, for example, and protecting them from stress. Third, that we should indeed care about and cherish ourselves – be kind to ourselves, give ourselves occasional treats, experiences to savour. Fourth, that we should trust ourselves, so that when we come to take decisions we can rely on our own judgement and don't merely reflect the opinion of whoever we last talked to. This of course implies developing our own judgement – learning – and consulting our own judgement, listening to ourselves. And finally, that we should be able to do things, or simply be, on our own, that we should be able to enjoy our own company and not find it oppressive. Implicit in all of these is not only the requirement that we have a firm sense of self, but also that we develop a sort of empathy with ourselves, so that we listen to our own emotions, our own "vibes".

It may at first sight seem paradoxical to begin a discussion of how to make friends with other people by talking about making friends with oneself. It does however follow quite logically from what I have said in earlier chapters – about the importance of having a firm sense of self, for example. Thus if our self-esteem is low, it is often impossible for us to imagine that other people will think highly of us. We automatically ask, unconsciously if not consciously, "Why should they feel I'm worth spending time with, or talking to, or giving to, or caring about?" In other words, we distrust their motives. They will almost certainly pick this up quite quickly, and equally quickly get fed up with it. We tend to ask for reassurance, but in a back-handed fashion, saying things such as: "Oh, I'm sure you don't really want me to come along, I'll only get in the way." Not wanting to be unkind, they probably reply, "Don't be silly, of course we want you to come", while in reality thinking the exact opposite. Since people tend to resent being distrusted and being pressurized like that, and being forced to behave dishonestly, they will probably lose no time in distancing themselves from us as far as they can. So our distrust becomes a self-fulfilling prophecy: our low self-esteem sets up a vicious circle in which our behaviour has the effect of keeping it low, or even of lowering it still further.

My starting point, then, is ourselves, and not some list of "ten tried techniques for making friends". I do not regard friend-making as a skill to be taught, in the way that air hostesses are taught to smile or insurance salesmen are taught to sell insurance. While there are certainly some techniques to be learned – how to become aware of other people's feelings, for example, and how to avoid behaving in ways that pressurize them – the fundamental skill is that of becoming the sort of person that other people respect and want to be friends with. So we have to attend to our own self-image and self-esteem, make friends with ourselves. Once we have made a start on this, we have taken the first step in setting up "virtuous circles", in which our behaviour is attractive to other people rather than off-putting, and so helps to strengthen and reinforce our self-image and self-esteem.

Let me try to be more specific. I argued in the chapter on "Attraction" that one at least of the ingredients of attraction is some mysterious psychological chemistry, which presumably we can't do a great deal about. And no doubt there are methods of attracting people which we don't want to employ – such as advertising our sexual availability, or just being "a soft touch" – because they would attract 'the wrong sort of person'. But I believe that a significant element in determining whether or not we attract other people is the extent to which we put up barriers around ourselves, wall ourselves up against other people. Some of us, it is true, find ourselves attracted to walled-up people, rather like a moth to a flame, and with similar unfortunate results. But in the main, being walled-up is not an effective way of attracting people, certainly not of attracting them into a lasting friendship.

Why do we wall ourselves up? As we saw in the chapter on "Sense of Self", it seems that we do need to have a fairly clear idea of where the boundaries of our various domains are, but if we feel insecure, if we lack confidence in our autonomy, if we fear what will happen if other people can invade our privacy and get to know too much about us, we are liable to turn these boundaries into walls – fortified, in extreme cases, with barbed wire and watch-towers. Not only do these walls keep other people out, they keep our own selves in. That is to say, they prevent us from revealing ourselves to other people. Reluctant to reveal our negative feelings – our fears, anxieties and vulnerabilities, or bottled-up aggression or anger – we also conceal our positive feelings – our concern, our tenderness, our love. Eventually we reach the stage where we conceal these things even from ourselves. It is these self-same walls, of course, that get in the way of our empathizing with other people. The obstacles to empathy described in the chapter on

"Empathy and Rapport" all act as barriers, or walls, that prevent other people's messages from reaching us. And once again, the lesson is that if we are to be able to lower these walls, we must come to terms with our negative feelings. Only if we are strong enough within ourselves will we be able to choose to do without walls. What we must do, then, is to strengthen our sense of self. Hence the necessity of doing something about that, whether by reading books like those by Anne Dickson, Dorothy Rowe, and Muriel Schiffman, which are mentioned in the chapter on "Sense of Self", and acting on the advice they give, or seeking professional help from an experienced counsellor, or trying out some kind of individual or group therapy.

I would like to lay some stress here on *choosing* to do without walls. I am not suggesting that we should go around "letting it all hang out", revealing everything about ourselves to all and sundry at the drop of a hat. What someone with empathy and a strong sense of self will usually have is a basic "stance" that favours self-revelation: they will regard it as normal and healthy, which people who don't have a strong sense of self will not do. But this preference for self-revelation will be exercised judiciously, not indiscriminately: it will be exercised with *judgement* – a sense of how much, where and to whom self-revelation is appropriate; a sense, indeed, of who would be a good friend to them and who would not. (This, of course, implies too an awareness of how they and others interact.) The need to develop this kind of judgement is really important: indeed, it is sufficiently important to have the status of basic principle number two for making friends.

Looking outwards now towards other people, and again using the chapter headings of Part Two as a checklist, we can draw out further principles to guide us in our approach to making friends. Our friends must be people whom we accept and respect, and who accept and respect us. This implies taking each other seriously, not condescendingly or patronizingly, and adopting a basic stance towards one another that is accepting rather than judging. We relate as equals, rather than one of us taking it upon himself or herself to judge the other. So if, say, our friend habitually annoys us by being a few minutes late for meetings, we react not by pronouncing him or her guilty of disrespectful behaviour and breach of contract – "I've taken the trouble to be here on time, why can't you?" – but by explaining what feelings their lateness produces in us and what we propose to do (exercising our autonomy) to limit the annoyance that we feel: take something to read while we're waiting; not wait longer than fifteen minutes; not agree to rendezvous on noisy, windswept street corners; have custody of our own ticket if we're going to a performance of some kind, so that we don't have the anxiety of wondering whether our friend will be late and we shall consequently miss the start.

The next principle is to do with the obligations of friendship. It says that obligations should be arrived at by mutual understanding or by our assuming them voluntarily, not by one or other imposing their expectations or claiming "rights" or presuming on the other's goodwill. One important thing that follows from this principle is that it sets limits to the responsibilities that we take upon ourselves – limits, that is, to what obligations we assume – because we do not have to be bound by any expectations or claimed rights or presumptions on the part of our friend. I would argue, though, that there are two kinds of responsibility that we *should* voluntarily assume. If at any time our friend appears to be under a misapprehension about the obligations that we feel towards him or her – that is to say, if they think they stand in relation to us somewhere other than where we would place them – it is our responsibility to correct this misapprehension, to tell them honestly where they stand, and not let them continue to labour under a delusion. And secondly, we should accept that we are responsible for the emotions that deliberate or thoughtless actions on our part induce in our friend, and therefore accept an obligation to do what we can to mitigate them if they are

119

distressing or damaging. Emotions which we trigger off but could not reasonably have anticipated – for example, because they have their roots deep in our friend's psychological make-up – are a different matter. We cannot reasonably be expected to take responsibility for arousing them: it is fundamentally our friend's own responsibility to deal with them, although it would be a friendly act to offer help if we can.

My final principle is to do with honesty versus pretence. The need to be honest with ourselves in appraising our own strengths and weaknesses, so that we may appreciate the former and face up realistically to the latter, is central to the process of developing a firmer sense of self. We will get nowhere, with ourselves or in our relationships with other people, if we pretend that we have strengths which we don't have, or that we don't have weaknesses which we do. We need too to be honest when we think about and analyse our relationships: we need to be *honestly* aware of how we interact with other people. Are those whom we call our friends actually *good* for us? Do we gravitate towards people who are so "prickly" that the demands they make upon our sensitivity are so great as to drive out the spontaneity of which we are capable? Is it the challenge that they present that attracts us, perhaps despite receiving little warmth or tenderness from them? Exactly what *are* our feelings towards those whom we call our friends? Is it attraction, a genuine liking, that makes us ring someone up, or just habit, or just loneliness, so that we simply have to talk to *somebody*? How strongly do we care about and cherish them? Are there limits to how much trust we would happily place in them? Are we genuinely able to give to them and receive from them without being tempted to view it as part of a transaction? It may be difficult for us to face these questions and answer them honestly, but if we can make the effort we are likely to find that it gets rid of a lot of confusion and the anguish that often accompanies it. I am not suggesting that we should be intolerant of what seem to us to be our friends' foibles and limitations, just that we should be honest with ourselves about their effect on us. And if we conclude that we don't *feel* close to them, we should not, in our behaviour towards them, pretend that we do.

15

First Encounters

Many friendships grow out of relationships that already existed, like being neighbours with someone, or workmates, or fellow-members of some club or society. Others, however, grow out of "first encounters", when people are introduced or bump into one another, as at parties, or in a bus queue, or sharing a table in a cafe or restaurant, or when they meet through some means like a marriage bureau or "lonely hearts" advertisement. What do such encounters require of us, and how can we make the most of such opportunities for starting a friendship?

If a first encounter is to lead on to a friendship, the first thing we need is the appropriate emotional equipment – some capacity to empathize with other people, sufficient sense of our own self to allow us to reveal something of that self to other people, and a degree of preparedness to accept other people and to be caring, trusting and giving. We also need some ability to think about the experience and learn from it. None of this equipment needs to be highly developed and sophisticated: just so long as we've got a bit of everything to start with, we will find that they grow with each encounter and all sorts of other interactions that we have. And secondly, we will need to bear in mind, of course, the basic principles that I talked about in the previous chapter.

Here is a little exercise to give an opportunity to begin to use that equipment and apply those principles. You have decided to answer a lonely hearts advertisement in a magazine. Would you

(1) Write very briefly, on the lines of "I saw your ad, perhaps we might like one another, here's my phone number"?

(2) Send a photocopied standard letter about yourself, talking about your achievements and putting yourself in the best possible light?

(3) Write a letter that takes up what's in the ad – an interest in music or politics or whatever – and gives a fair amount of information about yourself, touching on, for example, your history, or things that you enjoy, and why, as well as a basic physical description?

Now imagine yourself in the position of the person who placed the ad. Which reply would you prefer to get? If you can't answer this one without thinking about it, join me in trying to read between the lines. The three replies all contain, I suggest, a "hidden message":

(1) It is more important to me to protect myself, by withholding information, than to attract your interest.

(2) It doesn't matter all that much to me whether you reply or not, because someone else might. And anyway, if you don't I can always blame it on the fact that it's an obvious photocopy and so avoid having to ask whether there's something unattractive about me.

(3) I've "listened" to you, and even though you're unknown to me and I may never hear from you, I give you this information about myself. I am prepared to risk your knowing it and not responding.

Doesn't number (3) look like the best prospect for friendship? By a mile, I'd say.

In case it seems that this little exercise simply provides a "model answer" on which to base replies to lonely hearts ads, let me stress that it's not just a matter of technique. Unless we actually *want* to offer information, unless we actually *are*

123

prepared to take a risk, the chances are that what we say will not sound quite right, there will be a false ring to it, it will seem forced or contrived. The real lesson of this exercise is that fear of rejection, arising from low self-esteem, makes it more likely that rejection is what we'll get. Replies (1) and (2) were written with a fear of rejection behind them, and that is precisely what they courted.

In encounters at rather closer quarters, when we actually get to meet the other person, we can again follow the principles outlined in the last chapter: revealing ourselves to one another at a mutually agreeable pace, exchanging information, "unfolding" in step; not trying to manufacture obligations, nor allowing ourselves to be put under them: favours are not to be bought by an expensive dinner or a seat for a play. If we make material gifts, they are small ones, in recognition of the fact that the relationship is still at a very early stage. What we can give the other person, however are *opportunities* – to share equally in setting the "style" of the relationship, the rules about opening up and about physical closeness; to share equally in decisions, such as what to do of an evening; to say "no" to some suggestion of ours without fear of unleashing angry words or tight-lipped withdrawal. These are "gifts" that show that we accept and respect their individuality and autonomy. The deeper ingredients of friendship – trust, caring and cherishing – will, if they develop, do so over a period of time: they are more likely to do so if in the early stages we pay attention to those others that I have mentioned.

We can, I think, draw from these principles some guidelines about how to behave in first encounters. I would emphasize that these guidelines are not techniques to enable you to manipulate other people or ingratiate yourself with them: their purpose is to allow you to be relaxed and at your ease, and to put others at their ease, so that you can do things together, talk and interact without strain or affectation – enjoy yourselves, no less.

1. Think of your encounters – past, present and future – as *opportunities to learn*, which is what they are. There is no need to think of them as tests or ordeals. If that is how they seem, it is because you have chosen to view them that way.

2. Be aware of the "etiquette" of the situation, the set of rules about what is and is not polite behaviour. Some of these you surely know already, like "Don't pick your nose when talking to someone" and "Don't ask someone to whom you've just been introduced intimate questions about their sex life". Others are more subtle, to do with things like not standing too close to someone who is talking to you. If you do find it difficult to gauge appropriate distances, or indeed if you ever feel when you're with other people that you're involved in a game but don't know what the rules are, then you need some help and tuition.

3. Create opportunities for other people to talk with you. At parties, for example, you might try standing near the food and drink: some of the best parties take place in the kitchen. By all means experiment with sitting on a chair pushed back into a corner by itself, and avoiding eye-contact with other people, but I would be surprised if you wanted to repeat it. Make it easy for other people to start a conversation with you, and you with them. *Give* them, and yourself, that opportunity.

4. Put stereotypes out of your mind. This means not judging by appearances – not judging whether someone is worth talking to by how they look or how they dress. And don't think of yourself in stereotyped terms either – "I'm a highly paid lawyer, people should treat me with respect", or "I've only just left school, how can anybody find me interesting?" Stereotypes are barriers to mutuality in conversation.

125

5. Give clear signals. When you catch someone's eye, and you want to talk to them, signal that fact by allowing yourself to nod or smile, rather than putting them in the position of having to guess whether you'd like to talk to them or not. Similarly, if you're offering a hand to shake, hold it out: don't let it hover at hip level while you're wondering whether the other person will want to shake hands with you. Watch out for unclear or conflicting signals given by other people, and be very wary of them (the people and the signals). Someone who touches you while talking to you might *not* be signalling that they'd welcome a sexual advance, especially if they come from one of the Mediterranean countries, for example, where touches are a normal accompaniment to – indeed part of – conversation. To you their signals might be conflicting, to them they're not. The greeting and farewell kiss is another gesture that may cause trouble through being misunderstood. Is it bestowed out of convention, like a handshake? Or does it indicate liking, or sexual attraction, or perhaps reveal a need on the part of the giver for reassurance that he or she is a socially acceptable or sexually attractive person? If you're on the receiving end, you may not be able to tell which if any of these is the case, nor whether it indicates that you are somebody special, though you may learn something by observing whether everybody else receives the same gesture.

6. Take risks. Reveal yourself. Make eye-contact, say hello. *If you're snubbed, it's the one who snubs who is the social incompetent, not you.* True, you're exposing a "need" to be acknowledged: we all have that need, and anyone with an ounce of sensitivity responds to it when they see it in someone else. Someone who snubs may be having an off-day; alternatively, they may actually not have anything to give in friendship, even if they do have an ability to look

126

bright and make small-talk at parties. But don't jump to the conclusion that you have been snubbed: it could be that they were engrossed in somebody or something else at the time and simply didn't notice you.

7. Give other people choices. At parties, don't corner them: give them the chance to circulate if they wish. Don't make it embarrassing for them to break off the conversation: allow little pauses that they can take advantage of. If they go off for food or a drink, don't indicate that you expect them to come back now and resume the conversation. But if you have enjoyed talking to someone, tell them. (And let your smile show your appreciation when they do come back!)

8. Respect other people's autonomy and boundaries. When talking with them, be alert for sensitive "no-go" areas, and don't push. For example, if someone conspicuously refrains from responding to a "cue" of yours – perhaps you've touched on a matter of sex, religion or politics and they've abruptly changed the subject – don't return to it and try to probe.

9. Don't treat verbal challenges as threats. Your sense of self will be threatened only if you let it be. It is true that some people do have a challenging style: by way of response you need do no more than wonder to yourself whether they find that such a style helps them to make friends and influence people. It could be, of course, that behind the challenging manner there is a shy and insecure person who's determined to conceal that fact. If you can respond by standing your ground but not being challenging in return, there's a chance that they might later begin to relax their defences and allow their real qualities to show through.

10. Give other people opportunities – they have the choice whether to accept them or not – to reveal themselves. Do

this not by remorseless probing, but by inviting disclosure in a way that gives them control over how much they disclose. So you can ask questions such as "Do you enjoy living where you do/your work/Christmas/...?", "Do you miss ...?", "Would you do it again ...?", "Are you looking forward to ...?" Ask questions according to whatever the conversation allows and is appropriate to the company; and when they reply, use your imagination – your empathy – to put yourself in their shoes. Allow yourself to warm to them. You will find yourself responding automatically, without thinking about it, in a way that keeps step with them. Thus are friendships born.

It is possible to have a perfectly pleasant and satisfying conversation with someone, a conversation that you both enjoy, then to say goodbye and go your separate ways. Before deciding that you want to see them again, and making the suggestion, you owe it to yourself and them to be clear about your motives. It is important to be honest. Are you being unduly influenced by a desire on your part to be liked, to win another person's approval? Do you want to "capture" them into your circle of friends? Is it their status or glamour that attracts you? Is your enthusiasm leading you to overlook danger signs? For example, were both of you being self-revealing, or just one of you? Did you come across significant no-go areas or signs of falseness or pretentiousness? What clues did you pick up about the other person's attitude to other people – their spouse, colleagues, friends, children (extensions of himself or herself, or individuals in their own right)? Do they respect other people or regard them with condescension? Were you able to be spontaneous, or was there a bit of you that felt anxious to please, or had that uncomfortable feeling of "walking on eggshells"? I stress these possible danger signs purely because they are the ones most likely to be overlooked, especially if you have found yourself responding spontaneously to the attractions and the promise. Remember that you have a choice – as does the other person too, of course. You are free to say, just as you would at a party: "It was nice meeting you. I have enjoyed talking to you. Goodbye." And you are equally free to say: "It would be nice to carry on the conversation some time." Then just see what response you get.

16

Developing a Friendship

No two friendships are exactly alike. The variety is infinite. So it is important to produce a set of specific guidelines about developing them that will apply to friendships in general. (First encounters, by comparison, come in a much more limited range of shapes and sizes.) What we can do, however, is to look at what's involved in "developing" a friendship, and see whether we can set down some key principles to bear in mind and be guided by.

In what ways, then, does a friendship "develop"? We find ourselves doing more and different things together, perhaps. Maybe we spend more time on them, and enter into each other's lives more and more, so that the respective "compartments" that the shared activity occupies in our lives widen and possibly overlap with other compartments, as we get to know each other's families and other friends. The boundaries of "our" compartment become more diffuse and less easy to pinpoint, but this doesn't matter so much as it did once, because we know each other well enough to have a tacit understanding about where they are – about whether we invite each other to family occasions, for example. Moreover, because our friendship is established we don't have to exert ourselves to defend it against the demands on our time and attention from other relationships and activities.

As a friendship develops we are also likely to find ourselves talking to each other and listening to each other more and more. (If we are talking and listening less and less it could be because we've got to know each other so well that we don't need words in order to communicate, but it is perhaps more likely to be because we've run out of things to say to each other: boredom has set in and the friendship has ceased to develop.) More talking and listening is likely to involve more confiding: we reveal more of our selves to each other, and there are fewer no-go areas so far as conversation is concerned.

Doing more things together, and more talking and listening, are the visible, surface signs of a developing friendship. Our attitudes towards one another, and our feelings about one another, change as well. We learn to trust each other more, in all the various senses of the word, as our experience of each other grows. (We also learn, perhaps, how far we can trust each other – what the limits are. There may, for example, be some temptations to which we learn not to expose our friend, but that does not mean to say that he or she is generally untrustworthy, not a good friend.) We find ourselves more prepared to give and receive, we care about and cherish each other more deeply. Our feelings of rapport with each other come more strongly and more deeply. As time passes the mutual obligations between us grow: we learn where we can depend on each other, what expectations of each other it is safe to have. Sometimes, though, obligations creep up on us, and we may come to feel trapped by them, as in the case where you and your friend have spent the last five Christmases together, and he or she takes it for granted that you will do the same next Christmas.

There are, I think, other and more subtle ways in which we change as a friendship – a *real* friendship – develops. Our empathy grows. We find that we sense more readily what each other is feeling, and that it is easier to imagine ourselves in their shoes. We may find that we have a greater capacity to empathize not only with our friend but with other people as well. Ideally, our sense of self develops too. Although in some circumstances friends find themselves "merging" with each other – perhaps they remember how unsatisfactory their lives were before they met, and can't imagine being without each other in the future – in other relationships, which I consider to be healthier ones, doing things together, talking and listening to each other, trusting, giving and receiving, caring and cherishing, all serve to reaffirm the status of each of us as a free-standing individual in his or her own right: our self-image becomes clearer and more distinct, our self-esteem is raised.

It seems to me that in many ways empathy and sense of self are the "keys" to friendship. On the one hand, the greatest rewards of friendship are that our empathy is enhanced and that our sense of self becomes firmer. On the other, the most important things that we can do to help a friendship develop are not to press our friend to do more or to talk more, but for us to help each other to dissolve the obstacles to empathy that are within each of us, and to foster the other's sense of self, while not forgetting to affirm our own. If we can accomplish this, everything else that marks the development of a friendship would seem to follow. What, then, do we need to do to accomplish it?

Let's start with empathy. First, how good are the two of you at picking up unspoken messages from the other, at sensing what's in or on their mind, what their feelings are at a given moment? If you sometimes are not aware what the other is feeling, is this because you aren't paying attention, or are you actually impervious to the messages that are being sent out? Clearly you *should* pay attention to each other, but that by itself is not enough: the one who feels that his or her messages are being ignored *must say so*, otherwise the other will never have the chance to learn how to recognize the signals and practise the skill until it becomes automatic, a taken-for-granted part of one's empathy mechanism. If you're the one who feels ignored, it may be very tempting to say to yourself, "Oh, he/she will never understand, it's a waste of time trying to explain". This will serve the dual purpose of saving you from having to try to explain (which is convenient if you feel vaguely guilty or uncomfortable about the thoughts that are in your mind), and of labelling the other as a stereotype – the non-understanding man or woman. It won't do the friendship any good, but it may assist you, while the friendship lasts, in "managing" it, because you can always relate to the other as simple stereotype rather than complex individual. Some husbands and wives tend to do this, but friends sometimes do as well if they come to feel threatened by closeness.

Another approach is to be conscious of, and to inspect, the feelings that your friend's behaviour produces in you. Are these ever, when you reflect on them afterwards, irrational or inappropriate? Do you, for example, find yourself feeling angry, or guilty, or embarrassed, or like a child, for what afterwards seems like no good reason? If so, these feelings will certainly get in the way of your empathizing with your friend. Their source may well lie in your childhood or adolescent (or even later) experience. To take an illustration, you're about to go away for a week or two to the other side of the country. Your friend says to you, "Will you phone me?", and all of a sudden you feel very angry towards him or her. Silly, really, but why did it happen? If you ask yourself what you felt immediately before the anger, maybe it was a feeling that you were being pressurized. And if you ask what that reminds you of, perhaps what comes to the surface is that when you left home for the first time, your parents were always on at you to phone them and tell them everything you were doing, as if even though you had left you had no right to lead your own life in privacy. Once you have identified that feeling and got it out into the light of day – and your friend can help you by pointing to the irrationality of your initial response – you will be able to regard it as nothing more than what it is, a useless hangover from the past, and it will cease to trouble you and get in the way of your empathy. Although your upbringing may have left you with a number of such "landmines" or "booby-traps" that your friend may innocently stumble over, a single explosion need do no damage if the two of you can deal with it coolly, and once you've dismantled the repeater mechanism it will be harmless.

Your emotions can also get in the way of your empathy if you tend to be preoccupied with your own self-esteem and how you appear to other people. If your friend says to you, "I'm unhappy" and your reaction is to say, "Don't blame me", it is clearly *your* feelings that are uppermost in your mind, not your friend's. Such a preoccupation seems to result from a general feeling of insecurity: if you are badly afflicted it can lead to you inspecting everything that is said to you to see whether it can be interpreted as threatening or blaming or disparaging. It will take a lot of tolerance on the part of your friend for him or her not to disappear into the distance. But if they will stay with you, and quietly make the point that they would appreciate a more constructive response, and if you can find it within yourself to make that constructive response, you may be on the road to learning that your self-esteem is not such a fragile thing that you need to be fearing for it all the time, and sacrificing your empathy in the process.

Let us ask now what friends can do to foster one another's sense of self. Sense of self, you may remember, I defined as being made up of our self-image – how we see ourselves – and our self-esteem – how we judge ourselves. Self-image in turn is made up of our sexual identity, our perceived abilities and qualities, our security, and our separateness. If our friend has any problem with sexual identity, we can respect his masculinity or her femininity by not questioning it or putting them in a position where they feel that they have to demonstrate it by conforming to social expectations – men to be tough and patronizing towards women, women to be "ladylike" and preoccupied with domestic concerns. As regards separateness, we treat our friend as an individual in his or her own right, not as somebody else's "other half" or dependant. We allow him or her to be themselves, and don't impose our expectations on them. As I said earlier, we don't require them to change the way they look, or the clothes they wear, or the opinions they hold, or the other company they keep, as a condition of their being allowed to be our friend. Far from merely tolerating our friend, we will *value* him or her, and demonstrate the fact. Thus we will invite and respect their opinions and judgements, will show our appreciation of their contribution to the relationship, and let ourselves be seen to relish and enjoy those things that we do relish and enjoy, and that make the friend distinctive and "special". We will respect their autonomy, by offering them freedom and choices in how they relate to us, by not presuming on their goodwill, by not insisting on holding them to proposals that they made in a moment of enthusiasm or intoxication and now regret, or by bringing pressure to bear on them to do what we want them to do. We will trust them. We will respect their boundaries by not muscling in and trying to run their lives for them. When we decide and do things together, "power" and responsibility will be shared equally. All of these things will naturally boost our friend's self-esteem as well as self-image, but we can help to reinforce the latter by offering encouragement and reassurance, not necessarily uncritically, whenever we see the need.

To end this chapter, it is worth mentioning some studies described by Michael Argyle and Monika Henderson, which discovered a wide agreement about how friends should behave towards one another. The most important "rules for friends" – important in the sense that if they were broken the friendship was most likely to break up – were the following: Don't be jealous or critical of your friend's other relationships; volunteer help in time of need; trust and confide in each other; don't criticize each other in public; show positive regard for each other; stand up for your friend in his or her absence; be tolerant of each other's friends; show emotional support; don't nag. Some of these are very much to do with feelings, and have already been discussed in this chapter, but they are all worth bearing in mind as guides to good practice, or etiquette, in developing and maintaining friendships.

17

Helping Your Friend to Cope

For the purpose of this chapter, let us assume that you are the friend of someone who is in a state of crisis, of emotional instability, with painful and alarming feelings bubbling up and spilling over in a way that he or she plainly finds difficulty in coping with. It may be that the state they are in has something to do with an important relationship in their life, involving their spouse or partner. Let us also assume that the relationship between you and your friend is a fairly straightforward one, a friendship not interwoven with heavy obligations and not involving complex psychological mechanisms. In this chapter I want to outline a six-step process by which, with some help from you, your friend could move from a position which is probably one of some desperation to a position where they feel able to take positive decisions to improve matters.

The first step is to provide the opportunity, in a warm and private environment, for your friend to talk, to confide in you. That he or she should trust you, and that you should be able to empathize with them, is clearly of paramount importance here. Note that at this stage it is not for you to probe or ask penetrating questions, and certainly not to pass judgements of any kind: just be sympathetic and "open". The very act of confiding will provide some release, as he or she expresses their distress, gets it off their chest. In confiding, they will describe what their feelings are, give names to them, relate them to other feelings that they may have had in the past, or have heard about or read about in works of fiction or real-life case histories. This is an important first step towards coping with and eventually, if possible, eradicating feelings that are painful and alarming. It is important, I think, that your friend should articulate what he or she has felt by describing the feelings that have been experienced, rather than in terms of some concept such as "needs". What we have inside us are feelings, not needs: we arrive at statements of what we need by reasoning or making intuitive leaps from our feelings: it is our feelings, not our needs, that are the basic starting point. Even the raw cry "I need my mother" stems from a feeling, that of being deprived. A statement beginning "I need ..." is already some way along the route from problem to solution. (In the first instance, of course, what "I need" is to be able to voice my feelings, and that is precisely where you, the friend, come in.)

To voice one's feelings is not only to describe them, to say what they are; it is also to express the intensity with which they are felt. Thus your friend may communicate feelings in a voice that conveys sheer anguish and panic. It is your job as their friend to share, and in part absorb, the feelings *but not the intensity*: it is for you to reflect back the feelings, but in a cooler and calmer way. It is most important, by the way, to let the anguish and panic, the distress, come out unimpeded. If your friend breaks down in tears, the message to give is "It's all right to cry"; *not* – repeat *not* – "Don't cry." Crying, like shivering or shaking or having a fit of the giggles, is in itself therapeutic: in the process we actually discharge some of the distress we feel. (On this subject, see *How To Change Yourself and Your World*, by Rose Evison and Richard Horobin.)

The second thing for you to do as your friend's confidant is to disentangle their story. The purpose of this is not only to inform yourself about what has happened, in order to be better able to help; in answering your questions about, for example, what the sequence of events actually was, your friend will gradually "distance" himself or herself from the experience and thereby be able to put it into perspective. At some point, although not until the intensity of the feelings has worn off a little, it will become possible to ask, "How do you think it looked from the other side?", and to do so without appearing to be partisan. But, I repeat, this is not a question to be asked in a hurry. You can come back to it later, after going through some of the following steps in the process. By the way, do note that the process is likely to have to be a reiterative one: that is to say, you and your friend may need to go through the cycle several times, perhaps with new bits of story coming out each time, before a satisfactory and stable version of events – one that "makes sense" – is arrived at.

Step three begins the analysis of what happened. The stress here is emphatically on analysing, on asking "Why?", and not on apportioning blame. To be able to say "It was his (or her) fault" may afford some satisfaction, but it is not constructive. It is probably not very helpful either to ask the "cause" of the flare-up (or whatever the problem is) – there is never a single "cause", and you're liable to find yourself back in the business of blaming. But you can try to pick out triggering events, in the absence of which the flare-up would probably not have occurred when it did or where it did in the form that it did. And similarly one can ask whether there were any crucial elements in the situation that formed the background to the events, crucial in the sense that if they had been absent or different then the course of events and the outcome would have been different. One can ask what choices were made, and by whom: what autonomy, what freedom of choice, did that person have? And it may also be very fruitful to ask whether there are any recognizable patterns in what happened, and whether the events followed a pattern that had been experienced in the past. For instance, does one partner never ask for something directly – for fear of refusal? or seeming pathetic? – but only indirectly, which then leads the other to feel manipulated and hence angry and unco-operative? Was it all in some dreadful way foreseeable, with both partners knowing what would happen but finding themselves in the grip of a seemingly inexorable process and powerless to do anything about it? Does either partner have standard defence mechanisms that regularly come into play when triggered off by certain kinds of action on the part of the other? What drives and motivations can reasonably be inferred to have been at work, from the evidence that is available? The answers to these questions and to any others that it occurs to the two of you to ask, as well as the very process of seeking the answers, will help your friend to make sense of what took place and to gain a better understanding of how and why both of the partners behaved as they did.

After some time has been spent on step three, your friend may be able to move on to take a cooler and more dispassionate view of the feelings that the flare-up produced. This is step four. It involves assessing the feelings that were expressed closer to the heat of the moment, in step one, and asking questions about them. It is particularly important to ask about feelings that now seem to have been out of proportion to the events and situation. Perhaps they were just surprisingly intense, maybe they were simply inappropriate. If your friend gets very defensive when talking about them, that is a sure sign that they were indeed out of scale or inappropriate. If the defensiveness persists, you should recognize that there is nothing more that you can do for the time being, except continue to be available if wanted. The important point about out-of-scale or inappropriate feelings is that they invariably cover up other, deeper feelings, as Muriel Schiffman argues. A feeling of anger, for example, may cover up a feeling of guilt or of wounded pride, or a feeling of envy may mask a feeling of shame. It seems that virtually any feeling – love, admiration, possessiveness, envy, anger, hate, rivalry, dependence or whatever – can mask any other. And a feeling towards one person may mask a feeling towards another. For example, you may be inordinately furious with someone your partner is attracted to because of inhibitions that prevent you from recognizing and coming to terms with the intensity of the anger that deep down you feel towards your partner: that anger may be very *frightening*, and so you displace it towards someone else.

You will never know in advance what questions to ask that will help your friend to uncover the concealed feelings. But questions like "When have you had that feeling before?" "What did that remind you of?" "What did you feel just before the anger overwhelmed you?" "Who else were you saying that to?" or "Why do you feel so strongly about...?" may have the effect of suddenly bringing them to the surface. When that happens, they will not so much be recognized intellectually as re-experienced, and that may be quite a fraught and dramatic moment, calling for all the sympathy and support that you're capable of.

By and large, covered-up feelings are ones that we literally do not want to admit to ourselves. This may be because we can't reconcile them with our self-image, and in particular our self-esteem. For example, our self-esteem may not allow us to accept that we were sometimes not good parents to our children, or sometimes not loved by our own parents. Alternatively, it may be that the triggering event or situation resurrects an ancient despair: it awakens memories of painful feelings that we have experienced in the past, feelings so painful that we have been covering up – repressing – both the memories and the feelings themselves. It may be tempting to explore covered-up feelings, but clearly this process may give rise to much pain. If your friend winces, you should not apply pressure. Remember that you are his or her friend, not their psychoanalyst or psychotherapist. What you can do, however, is to share your own knowledge and experiences with your friend. To know that there are other travellers on the same road can be uniquely reassuring.

At this stage, your friend may want to return to his or her "story". With the greater self-knowledge that they have acquired, things will now make sense that did not do so before. Events that previously seemed irrelevant will now have a place,

behaviour that previously seemed inexplicable can now plaus-
ibly be accounted for. To paraphrase Phillida Salmon, what is
happening now can be linked with what has passed, and linked
also to what may yet happen. So your friend can now begin to
look forward, and embark on step five in the process. What
opportunities exist for the person they now see themselves to
be? In what direction could they travel? What choices are open
to them? What needs to be done? Your role as their friend is not
to make recommendations, saying such things as "This is what
you've got to do...", but to serve as a sounding board, helping
your friend to examine his or her motives and the assumptions
behind the aspirations and hopes that they come up with, and
to explore the consequences of alternative courses of action.
You yourself could suggest – but diffidently, without advocating – possible actions. Something that you can helpfully do,
though, is to help your friend to think about *principles*. I shall
look at principles in more detail in the chapter on "Making
Friends With Your Spouse", but there are two which are
worth mentioning here.

First is the principle that one should always think in terms of
"journeying" rather than of a blueprint for some utopian "end
state", some "and they all lived happily ever after" scenario.
Whether it's a journey away from a current intolerable
situation, or a journey in the direction of greater happiness (an
aspiration, not a blueprint), there is really no realistic alternative, because no one has the power to decide by themselves
what form their relationships with other people will take in the
future: all that your friend can realistically take decisions about
is the steps that he or she individually will take. The second, but
allied, principle is that one should always make a distinction
between aspirations for oneself and the demands that one
makes of others. Certainly two partners may find that their
respective aspirations for themselves are in conflict, but the
way to resolve this conflict is by exploration first and open-
ended negotiation second: the moment that one partner says,

"I need you to do such-and-such", the whole enterprise is sunk. If you can help your friend to bear this in mind, you will be doing him or her a considerable service.

Now at last you and your friend are at step six, the final one. He or she has already been on a journey, with your company along part of the way. They might still be thinking in terms of needs, although probably they won't want to. They will think instead in terms of how their story will go forward – their aspirations for themselves, the choices that are open to them, the changes that they want to make in their lives. They are now ready and in a position to take decisions and act on them. You as their friend may still have a role to play, but if you have got this far you have already achieved a great deal.

Standing back from this account of how you can help your friend, we can see that the solution to the problem lay in restoring to them their sense of self, reminding them in particular of their autonomy, their freedom to take decisions about their own life. How did that autonomy come to be lost in the first place? It is clear that the repressed feelings within made them peculiarly vulnerable. The fact is that all of us have these vulnerabilities, but mostly we are able to keep them successfully hidden. Every now and again, however, and not only in the context of domestic partnerships, something happens that strips away the covering, exposing the raw nerve underneath. For example, you may suddenly find yourself completely and utterly thrown into confusion by receiving conflicting messages – such as, "come hither" *and* "keep your distance" – from someone of the opposite sex, because you are subconsciously reminded of receiving similar messages from your mother at a time when you were very small and totally dependent on her, and simultaneously and confusingly experiencing intense hate as well as intense love for her. Or if as a child you suffered a series of irregular, arbitrary and inexplicable abandonments by your parents, some event in your adult life may trigger off a fear that you are about to be abandoned that is quite overwhelming and again wholly out of proportion to the actual event: there may well be not the slightest rational justification for it at all. Or if you had to fight off your own parents to be able to lead your own life, an event may occur that leads you to feel – incomprehensibly to other people – invaded and intruded upon, and so you react in a fiercely defensive and distancing way. At such times we cease to behave as free-standing individuals, we don't realize our autonomy and our strength: we are driven by forces beyond our control, perhaps manipulated by other people. It is as if our past has installed in us strings which other people can twang: they can play a tune and make us dance to it. If we can survive our crises, with help from our friends, these strings will be cut, leaving us not where we were before the crisis but further along the road to self-fulfilment, to being genuinely free-standing individuals, in our own right.

18

Stress Between Friends

If you have read this far, you may be thinking that the picture
of friendship that I am painting is too idyllic to be true. That
would not be wholly fair, but I have certainly been emphasiz-
ing "real" friendship and trying to show its potential and what
it can achieve. In actual life, of course, no friendship is a totally
thorn-free bed of roses, or at least, not all the time. There are
bound to be stressful moments and periods in any relationship,
and friendships are no exception.

The symptoms of stress in a friendship can take many forms.
Perhaps something has happened to shake the trust that one of
you has in the other. Maybe one of you feels that you're not
getting the care and cherishing that you used to get, or that you
felt you deserved during a recent difficult time. There is the
feeling, perhaps, that all the giving is going in one direction,
and that one of you is rapidly exhausting the other's stock of
goodwill. Perhaps the empathy that used to be there doesn't
seem to be so any more, and misunderstandings keep occur-
ring. You feel that you're enmeshed in obligations that are
onerous, rather than giving you a reassuring feeling of knowing
where you stand. Or you're being presumed upon, your
autonomy isn't being recognized. These symptoms may have
been precipitated by various events, either within the friendship – an argument, perhaps – or outside it – one of you takes
up a new and time-consuming activity, or gets married, or
becomes a parent. So the one with more time on his or her
hands feels neglected, uncared for; the other feels guilty for
withdrawing and begins to resent the obligation that that guilty
feeling implies.

Sometimes friends who find themselves in this situation are able to talk to each other about what has happened and how they feel about it. All too often, however, they find they can't do that, and the breakdown in communication adds to the distress that they feel, prompting them to withdraw further and blame each other for their unhappiness: you're either behaving badly or being unreasonable. This progression is actually remarkably similar to that which occurs when a marital or other partnership breaks down. And it is plausible, to say the least, that the reason for this similarity is that the friendship has come to be marked – just like a partnership – not only by fuzzy boundaries, a lack of clarity about respective autonomy, and a muddle of obligations, but also by the usual psychological phenomena – transference, the deployment of defence mechanisms. Some of the uncomfortable feelings that the friends have may actually be inappropriate or irrational ones, like those that I discussed in the last chapter.

If the friendship has been going downhill for a time, proceeding inexorably like some of the matrimonial break-downs that many people nowadays have either experienced for themselves or seen their friends experience, then almost certainly the intervention of other people – mutual friends, or other friends or experienced counsellors who will help the friends individually to cope – will be called for if a final and irremediable split is to be averted. In some circumstances, such a sundering might be a good thing, just as dissolution is the best solution for some unsatisfactory marriages: in general, how-ever, because friendships are usually much less confining and constricting than marriages, it is probably a waste. Perhaps the best advice that one can give is: "Don't let your valued friendships slide downhill." This means *working* at them, and watching out for danger signs – in particular a falling-off of mutuality. If a friendship becomes progressively more one-sided, with one person doing the bulk of the giving and caring, or one always taking the lead in doing things together and the other always following, or one seeking the reassurance of obligations more than the other, then it is in need of attention. You need to talk to each other.

Unfortunately, it is a sad fact of life that the worse the state a relationship is in, the more difficult the people involved find it to talk to one another. And it is the one who is more unhappy who may find it more difficult to broach the subject: possibly he or she is the one with more at stake, more to lose, which may be how they came to be doing more of the giving and caring and following in the first place. Instead of talking, saying, "This won't do", he or she attempts to take advantage of their dependent position by structuring obligations, so that the less caring and giving one – the "leader" – will feel that he or she *ought* to reciprocate the giving and caring, etc. But the obligations tend to be resented, so this strategy is actually counter-productive, and the split between the two gets wider instead of narrower.

What is the solution? If you are the one in the dependent position, it is absolutely imperative that you reaffirm your own sense of self, that you remind yourself that you are an autonomous individual in your own right, and that you take responsibility for achieving your own happiness. Earlier I mentioned the expectations that can arise if you and your friend spent the last five Christmases together. Do *not* assume that you will spend the next one together as well. And, do *not* avoid mentioning Christmas plans until the end of November, so that if your friend tells you only then that he or she wants to go somewhere without you, they will be responsible for you being on your own, as it will then be too late for you to make alternative arrangements. If you can't conceive how you would spend Christmas without your friend, but he or she wishes to break the routine, the solution is not to manufacture an obligation for them, but to get conceiving, so to speak. Find out what your other friends are doing. Could you help serve Christmas dinner in the local hospital or hostel for homeless people, or switch your summer holidays to Christmas and go and learn ski-ing? Why not get in a supply of treats to read and eat, and decide that you're really going to enjoy your own company? Whatever you do, you must take responsibility for achieving your own happiness.

What if you're the one who feels depended on? Clearly you're already looking after your own happiness and don't need any urging to do so. What you may not ethically do, however, is to expect your friend (if that's really how you view him or her) to be there when you want them to be, and to take themselves off to suit your convenience when you don't. If in September you make plans to spend Christmas without your friend, but refrain from saying so until November – perhaps because it suits you to have him or her around during those two months – you actually *are* responsible for their ensuing unhappiness. It is your responsibility to be honest with your friend and with yourself, and to face up to the consequences for both of you of the decisions that you take. If you do not, you are not worthy of anybody's friendship.

Here is another scenario involving stress between friends. Consider the case where a disturbance to a friendship of yours is in the offing but has not yet occurred. Perhaps you have an opportunity to take up a new leisure activity or a more demanding job – an opportunity which, if you took it up, would lessen the amount of time and attention that you could give your friend and probably would get in return. If the loss seems to you to outweigh the benefits, assuming that you are able to make a calculation of that kind, it would logically follow that you would forgo the opportunity. It is important to note, however, whether you are basing the calculation on the assumption that the quality of the friendship is directly related to the amount of time that you spend together: is this necessarily the case? Is it not possible, for example, that you might spend less time in each other's company, but use it more positively and profitably? Perhaps it is due to habit and inertia, more than to anything else, that you spend so much time together now, pleasant though those periods are. Perhaps you could make more use of the telephone and letters to affirm and re-affirm your friendship. Might it not be that if the friendship could adapt to the change in your life, it would be deepened and enriched thereby?

Now let's turn the tables. Consider the situation where it is a friend of yours who has the opportunity to take up the new activity or job. How would *you* feel about it? Would you be resentful at the impending disruption to your friendship, and the prospect of having less of your friend's time? Would you have a sense of being abandoned, perhaps? Would you be genuinely pleased for your friend, while at the same time being upset to detect already a preoccupation with the new venture, a frame of mind to which your presence is scarcely relevant? Would you feel that you weren't being given the consideration that you were entitled to? Would you tend to react by sulking and withdrawing? Such feelings would, I think, be wholly understandable. But sulking and withdrawing hardly add up to a constructive solution.

An alternative approach might run along lines something like these. You could say to yourself: "This is giving me some very uncomfortable feelings. I'm feeling a bit hurt and a bit angry and very sorry for myself. (Possibly the situation is acting as a reminder of a similar situation in your past, which you mostly manage to keep safely buried, and so the pain is really out of proportion to what is happening now.) On the other hand, it's only natural for her to feel excited and a bit preoccupied: surely that's just how I would feel in the same position. More to the point, she is an autonomous human being, with the right to take her own decisions: the last thing I should be doing, as a friend, is bringing any sort of pressure to bear to influence that decision. It's not improper for me to say that I'll be sorry that we'll have less time together than in the past: it would be silly to try to appear indifferent. But I can also make it clear that my friendship won't be forfeited by her taking a decision that would involve seeing less of me in the future. On the contrary, she may have a difficult time ahead, and the least I can do is to assure her that my support will still, as in the past, be available if needed."

One of the most important things that one person can do for another is to uphold their autonomy – their freedom to take decisions, to take risks, to embark on changes without being pressurized or leaned on. (It is something that you will find it easier to do, incidentally, if you see *yourself* as someone with the right to autonomy.) It is for friends, then, to uphold one another's autonomy, and also – in the role of mutual confidants – to help one another to exercise that autonomy in a well-informed, thought about, and responsible way. If the outcome is that your feelings are hurt, then I'm sorry. But responsibility for dealing with your feelings lies in the last resort with you, not with your friend.

19

From Friend to Lover

A continuing friendship necessarily has a measure of stability.
The friends know where they stand in relation to one another.
Where they are of "complementary sexual orientation" – a
heterosexual man and woman, for example – but are not lovers
(i.e. there is no physical sexual relationship between them), this
may be because they have tacitly agreed that sex is out, or
because they have jointly decided it, or because one has decided
it and the other has accepted that decision. Whichever is the
case, there is a "line", and they both know where it is and take
its existence for granted. What happens if, one day, the
relationship does become a sexual one?

If one wanted to analyse how two friends happened to
become lovers, it would be necessary to look at a number of
factors. What were the motivations of each of them –
straightforward sexual desire? curiosity? a wish to be "close"?
to satisfy the desire of the other? Was there an absence of
restraints – some inhibitions removed by alcohol? others by the
availability of contraceptives? Had it been waiting for an
opportunity – time and a private place? What was the decision-
making or acting-upon-impulse process – was it planned
beforehand? spontaneous? did one pressurize the other? or you
just "turned each other on", did you? It is impossible to isolate
a single cause or reason. Motivations in particular are likely to
be complex and multi-faceted. Lynne Segal suggests that "it is
not some straightforward need for physical gratification which
motivates sexual behaviour and erotic desire, but rather, sexual
desire is knotted through with all sorts of other emotional needs
– to obtain approval and love, express hostility, dependence

and domination, relieve anxiety, and repair deep-lying psychic wounds of rejection, humiliation and despair." Equally complex may be the feelings that the two of them have afterwards – ranging in the first instance perhaps from a warm, cosy glow to wishing it had never happened.

But afterwards there may also be new attitudes, assumptions and expectations in the air. For instance, the man may now take on a very protective attitude towards the woman, perhaps out of instinct, or because it's his way of showing tenderness, or because he feels it's expected of him, and possibly there is an under-current of "ownership" mixed in as well. The woman, however, may find his attitude inexplicable and uncalled-for, or patronizing, and resent it. Either may, without giving much thought to it, take it for granted that they have new rights over the other – the right to know how they spend their time, and to have a bigger share of it, for example. If the woman has been socialized by her upbringing into thinking of herself as a sexual prize for men, she may assume that she is entitled to ask for privileges in return for surrendering her body. Thus each may seek to bind the other, but in the process something may be lost:

> He who binds to himself a Joy
> Doth the winged life destroy;
> But he who kisses the Joy as it flies
> Lives in Eternity's sunrise.
> William Blake, *MS Notebooks*

The "crossing of the line" therefore raises a number of questions, to do with personal autonomy and boundaries, the pattern of obligations between the couple, the implications for other parts of their lives (including other relationships, of course) and thus the nature and size of the compartment in the life of each of them that their relationship will occupy in future. "Where do we go from here? Do I want to do it again?

Regularly? Will I be expected to? Will it spoil the friendship if I don't? If I say I want the old 'line' back, will it look as though I found making love with him/her disappointing?"

To answer these questions, and to deal with the attitudes, assumptions and expectations that have surfaced, it is necessary to talk, to discuss, to negotiate. If you cannot find a new balance and restabilize the walls of your respective compartments, the friendship is doomed. You have to do this for yourselves: no book can help you. One guiding principle that you may care to adopt, however, is that it is the right of either of you to say "no more". You owe it to each other to consult, to deliberate and to explain, but the actual choice is one for each as an individual to take. If one says "no" and the other is disappointed, it is for the other to face up to the disappointment and to take responsibility for coming to terms with it. If the friendship cannot exist without sex as an ingredient, perhaps what you have found is that you have only a limited basis for friendship anyway. Although if two friends have also been lovers for a long time, and then one of them withdraws sexually, the other may find that very painful, with every moment spent in the company of the one who has withdrawn acting as a reminder of what once had been but now no longer is. Some people say that ex-lovers make the best friends, but maybe that happens only when the passion has died down on both sides – perhaps when both have found new lovers – and any wounds have had time to heal.

20

Making Friends With Your Spouse

Our relationships with our spouses, our marriage partners, are invariably much more complicated than those between us and our friends. Our lives are economically interdependent, in terms of "getting and spending"; we are embedded in a network of relationships that embraces our own children, if we have any, and the families that we and our spouse were born into; we operate in some contexts as a couple and in others singly; and we usually spend a lot of time together and have no obvious rules for rationing it. There will also be, as I have already mentioned, complex psychological processes going on between us, such as transference and the deployment of various defence mechanisms. As a result of these complications, we tend to relate to our partners not as individuals in their own right, but as if they were actors playing parts. So we treat each other as:

- "Functional" role-players: wage-earner, head of household, child trainer, cook, housekeeper, chauffeur, gardener

- Conferer of status, through occupation, social position, social connections, etc.

- Social stereotypes: macho, sensitive, liberated, super-woman, for example

- Power-holders, on whom we are dependent and to whom we are under an obligation: authority figures, holders of the purse strings

- Dependants, who depend on us and are under an obligation to us in return for our making provision for them

- Competitors – for the children's affection, the attention of other adults, for resources (time, money, etc.) to gratify their own interests

- Sexual objects

- Extensions of ourselves – so that we get embarrassed sometimes by things that they say or do, for example

- Triggers (unbeknown probably to them and to us) of concealed feelings – bearers of the "persona" of key figures in our earlier life.

The wonder surely is not that so many marriages break up, but that so many last!

In any marriage where the spouses treat one another in a number of these ways, there will be a corresponding range of obstacles to their achieving rapport; these obstacles will severely impede the growth and harmonizing of their respective capacities to empathize. And there will be obstacles too to each person developing and affirming their own sense of self.

What can we do to break out of a situation like this? In the first place, we can become *aware* of our position and of what's going on in the relationship. The best way to do this is to ask some questions. This isn't a book on marriage guidance, but here are some questions that you might like to ask yourself, and perhaps write down your answers:

- What is your "functional" role in your household?

- Do you ever feel that you exist only as half of a couple, and not as an autonomous person in your own right?

- Are you always trying to live up to your spouse's expectations of you (or what you think those expectations are)?

- Is it usually your spouse who takes the decisions in your household?

- Do you see yourself as having certain rights or legitimate demands, which it is your spouse's duty to satisfy?

- Do you, or would you, find it a bit threatening if your spouse has friends of his or her own, especially if you thought they might be talking about you?

- Are there areas of your life or emotions which it is important to you to keep your spouse out of?

- Are there resentments on either side that never get talked about?

- Do you know whether your spouse is happy in your marriage?

- Do you think your spouse would be able to guess accurately what your answers to the above questions are?

The second step in breaking out of the situation would be to put some effort in trying to follow the principles for making friends and developing friendships that I've talked about earlier. The result of your question-and-answer exercise may suggest to you that talking and listening ought to come high on the agenda, in which case one approach would be for both of you to do the exercise and then show each other your answers. If either of you reacts to that idea (or, if you get that far, to the other's answers) in a highly emotional way – if you feel very angry, or afraid, or insulted, for example – it needs to be recognized that this is not a rational or appropriate response to an attempt to discuss a relationship and the feelings that it produces. A highly emotional response indicates that there is some psychological block operating. If you can't sort it out on your own – and this is never an easy thing to do – *get help*. This would be the third step in breaking out. This help will have to come from outside, from a capable friend or a trained counsellor or therapist. The final step is to negotiate with each other – about your roles, the distribution of power, and so on. Actually, it's a good idea to do this *before* you get married. Discuss your expectations and hopes of life and each other, and try not to be so carried away by the excitement that you overlook anything significant; it could foreshadow a no-go area in the future. Don't forget to consider ways in which your circumstances could change in the future, especially if you have children. One thing that you might want to do is make a contract. This is particularly important for the one who is liable to find herself in a dependent position later on. The point about making a contract is not so much that you end up with a piece of paper that you can brandish at one another if you feel it's being flouted. It is the actual process of reaching it that is valuable in itself. It forces you to clarify what you want, it forces you to listen to what the other person says he or she wants, the two of you go through a joint, shared experience in negotiating it and putting it together, and – if you've done it in good faith – you emerge with a strong, shared commitment to upholding it. What you put in your contract is up to the two of you to decide, but it could cover:

– The sharing of domestic tasks, to do with the home and child-rearing

– The sharing of decision-making: neither of you to take important decisions without consulting the other – for instance, what to do if offered a better job in another part of the country – or you take turns in deciding what you do on holiday, say

– The expectations that you have of each other so far as your sex-life is concerned

- Budgeting. Will you have a joint bank account? (If not, is that because one of you doesn't trust the other, or feels that he or she should retain control over what they earn? Not encouraging signs.) Or will you have a joint account for shared expenses, but separate accounts as well, so that you don't have to ask if you want to spend some of "your own" money, with the element of autonomy that that implies?

- A commitment to communicate and negotiate generally on issues that arise in the course of day-to-day life. A useful book to read in this respect (it will also help with important decisions) is *How To Be A Couple And Still Be Free*, by Tina B. Tessina and Riley K. Smith.

Even if you didn't make a contract before you got married, it can be a useful exercise to think about what you would have put in it if you had had the chance, because this will help you to clarify what you want out of your marriage *now*. Explain politely to your spouse what you have been doing, and invite his or her collaboration in reviewing your relationship. It is your responsibility to broach the subject. If you do not do so, but instead complain that your spouse should have noticed without being told how unhappy you were, those to whom you complain may conclude, rightly, that you were either frightened to speak out or that it actually suited you to have a grievance to complain about and nurture. They may also conclude that neither explanation does you much credit.

If your spouse, or potential spouse, is antagonistic to the idea of a contract between you, you will want to take that information into account in deciding in which direction your future happiness lies, and what steps you are going to take towards it. If he or she responds positively, however, and your empathy enables you to reach an agreement firmly based on mutuality, you will find that you now have a partnership which will foster not only rapport between you but also your and your spouse's sense of self, your identities as distinct and separate persons. And thus you will find yourselves following the advice about marriage given by the philosopher, Kahlil Gibran:

And stand together yet not too near together:
For the pillars of the temple stand apart,
And the oak tree and the cypress grow
not in each other's shadow.

Kahlil Gibran, The Prophet

21

Making Friends With Your Child

If you are the parent of a young child, there are bonds of many kinds between you. A good deal has been written about these bonds, especially about those between a mother and her baby, and the extent of the infant's dependence on the continuous care of his or her mother if they are not to suffer "maternal deprivation". One of the most important bonds, however, has received very little attention, and that is the *power* that the parent has over the child. If, as your son or daughter grows up, you wish the relationship between you to become one of friendship, you must willingly relinquish that power. Friendship is a mutual and reciprocal relationship, between equals; thus it cannot coexist with a power relationship.

Parents exercise their power over their children in all sorts of ways. For example:

- We dish out rewards and punishments, thereby conditioning them to want to gain our approval and to fear our disapproval. We call this training. It gives us the excuse, if we want it, to be cruel for their own good.

- We take decisions on their behalf – for instance, what food they shall eat, what clothes they shall wear.

- We coerce them. We stand over them while they do what we want them to do – eat their tapioca pudding or do their homework.

- We intrude into their lives. If we know what they're up to –

what they're doing and what they're thinking – we can control it.

- We confuse them. For example, we don't practise what we preach (there's one rule for them and another for parents) or, having conditioned them to seek our approval, we screen our emotions from them so that they don't know whether what they're doing is approved of or not, and they withdraw, cowed. Sometimes we confuse them by schooling them in wishful thinking, so that they're unable to tell the difference between the likely and the improbable.

- We manipulate them. We instil guilt complexes, which we then play on. "How could you shame your parents like that?" "Oh well, if you're too busy to give me a hand ..."

- We foretell doom. "If you don't ... eat your spinach/save your pocket money/work for your exams ... you'll be sorry." (There's a manipulative optional extra: "... when I'm dead.")

If you are to become friends with your child, you must forswear the coercive, confusing, manipulative and doom-foretelling techniques from the start, and the others as soon as you can. Clearly, when your child is very young there is no alternative to taking decisions on his or her behalf and training them not to do dangerous things. But you can teach by example and explanation, you can allow your child to make and learn from mistakes (ask yourself, when tempted to interfere, "Do I *really* have to?"), you can share your own experiences and be liberal with your love, encouragement and reassurance, so that he or she will, for instance, happily tell you what's been going on at school, without you having to pry. The key aim must be to foster your child's autonomy, and respect it.

Even at the toilet training stage, you can allow your child the privilege of making a "gift" of his or her products rather than punishing them if they do not perform as you require. If you want to discipline your two-year-old not to interrupt the grown-ups' conversation, first discipline yourself not to interrupt his or hers, or indeed to stop any other activity in mid-flow: learn to say, "Excuse my interrupting, but it'll be dinner time in five minutes." If the child interrupts you, explain what is preoccupying you and say that when you finish it you will give them your full attention – and do so. If it's a rule of your house that your teenagers tell you beforehand when they want to bring a friend home, tell *them* when *you* want to do so. When your children, of whatever age, challenge the rules that you make, explain why you think they're needed – and if, in doing so, you begin to wonder whether they really are needed, be prepared to discuss the subject. Accustom your children to participating in family decision-making, and to taking their own decisions as far as possible. If they seem about to do something silly, you could say: "Look, I certainly don't know everything, but my experience leads me to think that if you do that there will be these consequences . . . I think you ought to be prepared to listen to advice from me or anybody else before deciding what to do. But if, after listening to me and considering what I have said, you decide to do something that I disagree with, I will respect your right to take your own decision and I will support you even though I disagree with you."

Also on the positive side, you can respect your children's privacy, their boundaries, and make it clear that you expect yours to be respected too. Even if your home isn't big enough for them to have rooms of their own, they can have minds of their own. You can trust your children, and show that you yourself can be trusted. Remember, though, that trust takes time to build up: if you've never trusted your children up to now, don't expect them not to take advantage of you at first when you start. You can reveal your emotions to your children (although some, like those to do with your sexuality, you may want to keep to yourself), and thereby help them to learn empathy, as well as how to cope with those emotions. Bear in mind that playing power games breeds resentment and concealment, both of which are enemies of empathy. And you can be caring and cherishing, as your parental instincts would probably lead you to be in any case. You would also need to find ways of helping them to resist pressures from people that they go around with – their peer group – and to cope with the insensitive, manipulative, untrustworthy people that they will meet in the world outside – ways, that is, other than becoming insensitive, manipulative and untrustworthy themselves. You will need to teach by setting an example, and by discussing your own experiences, those of others and those that your child has. And when your child has a bad experience at school, say, you will be able to respond not only with sympathy and support but with constructive advice about how to handle the situation.

You will not get it right all the time. The day will come when your child tells you what he or she expects *you* to do, puts you in your place. If your child can do that, and you can accept it, with gentleness and good humour, you will have become friends.

22

Making Friends With Your Parents

Just as there may be a strong and one-way power relationship between you and your child, so too may there be between you and one or both of your parents. If you have grown up on the receiving end of some or all of the techniques of exercising power that I listed in the last chapter, then your parents may well be "addicted" to using these techniques to control you, and you may be highly sensitized to them: when they twitch the string there's an answering jerk. Even without any exertion on their part, what you do in life may be governed by a desire not to wound them or hurt their feelings, or by the fear of how they would react if they knew what you were doing. In such a situation it is virtually certain that neither of you will have the capacity to empathize with the other, with a consequent and irremediable absence of rapport between you. You will certainly not be friends.

Do your parents go on about their "rights", or what old people or parents are "entitled to", or try to extract from you promises to visit or phone them or do things for them, or accuse you of not caring, or drop hints like "It's a bit much when other people look after you better than your own children do"? If they talk in these terms, it is a clear indication that they see their "problem" as being how to control you – how to exert power over you – rather than how to make the most of their own resources, or how to cope with particular difficulties. Unfortunately this attitude is totally counter-productive: it achieves quite the opposite effect to what they intend insofar as attracting loving care from you is concerned, as you know only too well. Even if it does have the effect of making you feel obliged to fulfil some of their expectations – and in the process satisfies them that they do still have some power over you – you probably do so resentfully and with bad grace.

If your parents are elderly, it is important to point out – even at the risk of making you more sensitive to them than you already are – what happens to people in old age in our society, what the prevailing attitudes to old age are, and how as a consequence the elderly see themselves.

As Phillida Salmon reminds us, "An old person no longer holds that passport to social recognition and social respect – a job. In family life, they are likely to be denied a responsible role in a household in which the young grow up." Elderly people living on their own, relatively immobile and with a reduced income, may find it difficult to organize social contacts to replace those that they have lost, and they become isolated and lonely. Others find themselves consigned to institutions, with a consequent loss of personal identity and autonomy. Cut off from the world, both groups become "strangers" in their own society, a society in which it is adulthood that is accorded much the greatest power and prestige. Old age is a decline from this peak or plateau, the elderly are "other" and "less". We focus on their incompetence rather than their competence. The "official psychology", as Phillida Salmon describes it, written by people who are not themselves old, portrays them in terms of deficiency and personal deterioration. We disparage their physical embodiments – wrinkled skin, faltering movements, shaky voice and hands. Busy young adults seem to disengage themselves psychologically from the old, who symbolize the transience and impermanence of their potency and vitality. And thus the elderly come to see themselves as "past it" or "useless". They may feel isolated from other people but at the same time dependent on them; they may feel painfully alienated from their own physical selves.

Some elderly people, however, may resist the denigration that this process implies. But in seeking to resist it, they may seize on the exertion of control over their children as one of the few things in life that it actually remains open to them to do: if they are successful it reassures them that they are still a force in the world, someone to be reckoned with. Certainly this is painful for you, their child, but at least they're not knuckling under: they retain some conception of their own identity even if they are trying to express it through you.

What can you do if you want to transform such a relationship into a friendship? In the first place, you can affirm your own sense of self – your separateness, your autonomy and your boundaries. You can take a decision, preferably at a time when you're in a calm frame of mind, about what you are prepared to give, in terms of time, attention, etc., and stick to it. Be gentle, but firm. Secondly, you can ask yourself what particular kinds of behaviour on your parents' part "get on your nerves", producing a strong reaction in you. It may be an irrational or inordinately strong reaction, a reaction appropriate to the young child that you once were rather than to the adult that you now are. Find out by talking to other people who have the chance to observe you or who have the same sort of problem but are triggered off by different kinds of behaviour. If possible, get one of your friends to help you to cope, to see what the underlying feeling is. If you can be aware of what is going on inside you, you will be well on the way to desensitizing yourself – you will no longer jerk when that particular string is twitched. Your parents will have to find, with your help, an adult way of getting you to do things for them – like bringing themselves to say "please" instead of taking it for granted that you will feel under an obligation to do what you're told.

As well as affirming your own sense of self, you should also try to foster your parents' sense of self. Although at first sight this may seem hardly necessary, the point is that they need to be able to affirm their own sense of self in other ways besides controlling you. Look for and respect the competence that they still have, rather than mourn that which they have lost. Let the practical help that you give them be in a form that they choose, if that can be managed, and of a kind that will extend their choices and opportunities in life, enabling them to maintain their dignity, self-respect and interests. More difficult, perhaps, but also potentially more fruitful, try to find a way of involving them in your life that allows you and your own children to continue to absorb something of the heritage that they carry and of what is valuable in their perspectives and personal qualities. To achieve this it may be necessary for you to negotiate – in just the same way as you might with your spouse – a "contract", to replace the set of assumptions and expectations about the parent–child relationship under which you grew up.

For you to be able to negotiate a "contract" several things are necessary. You must have a common language: each must be able to hear and understand what the other is getting at. You must both be prepared to look at your relationship and be willing to contemplate changes. You must both be prepared to accept the criticism that is implicit in another person's desire that you begin to do things differently. You must be able to talk in terms of "reasonable wants" rather than of duties and entitlements. And you must have in common at least some basic values and attitudes towards other human beings.

Sometimes there will be no hope of meeting these conditions. You may be so hypersensitive to your parents that you can tolerate them only in small, infrequent doses. Your parents may be temperamentally incapable of contemplating change. They may have devoted all their energies in the past to becoming skilled and adept performers in the art of making other people feel guilty and sorry for them, not least by making themselves thoroughly miserable even when the means of improving their lot are within their own grasp – to such an extent, indeed, that they can now conceive of no other way of relating to you. They may be snobbish, racist and greedy, whereas you are a conscientious inner-city social worker (or vice versa), with the result that some of your fundamental attitudes are diametrically opposed.

But few cases are quite so extreme, I suspect. One useful indicator is whether your parents are able to relate normally to other people of your own age. If they are, the problem is likely to be nothing more than that they – and perhaps you – are stuck in a rut of obsolete assumptions and expectations. If together you can extricate yourselves, you may well find that you are on the road to a rich and mutually rewarding friendship, together.

23

Finally ...

I have already said virtually everything that I can think of that seems to need saying, so this concluding chapter will not be a long one. I want to use it specifically to highlight and draw together some of the main themes that have emerged.

Perhaps the most important of these themes is that if we want to improve our ability to form and sustain friendships we must take steps to lower the walls, the barriers, which we erect in order to protect our vulnerable inner selves. These protective walls get in the way of our empathizing with other people – we tend to judge people rather than warm to them – and make it difficult for anyone else to relate to us: people cannot relate to something that is hidden from them. These walls also require a lot of energy to patrol and keep in good repair, and even then we can never really relax behind them. It's not necessary, nor indeed desirable, to get rid of them altogether: everyone needs at least a little railing to mark out their territory. But we do need to lower these walls, and to make a start on this we must do three things. In the first place, we must become aware of the walls that we have, we must know that they're there; even if we achieve no more than that, some of them will shrink simply by virtue of our realizing that they serve no useful purpose, that they are merely habits that we've got used to, and that they have the effect of putting off people whom we would like to attract.

Increasing our self-knowledge is not enough, however. The second thing that we need to do to begin to lower our walls is to make a positive effort of will, to summon up the resolve and the determination to do it. The aim is to move towards a basic stance, an attitude of mind, that is one of self-revelation rather than self-concealment. This means learning to take it for granted that we reveal, rather than conceal, ourselves. It means becoming accustomed to doing it automatically, so that it's concealment, not revelation, that has to be justified as a departure from the norm. If that involves undoing years of conditioning on your part, it won't be achieved overnight, of course. And inevitably such a change, even if it involves no more than careful little experiments at first, carries risks. But greater self-knowledge will help us to be more daring. And the risks will be minimized by the third thing that we need to do, which is to strengthen our sense of self.

The point about strengthening our sense of self is that if we can achieve this it won't actually need walls to protect it. For men in particular, this may involve strengthening their sense of security; for women, strengthening their sense of personal autonomy. It is possible to get trained help in doing this: for example, we can avail ourselves of some form of therapy or counselling (perhaps directed in the first instance towards some particular anxiety or difficulty), or get ourselves some kind of assertiveness training. But we can also do much to strengthen our sense of self by developing the friendships that we already have and forming new ones. This isn't as paradoxical as it may sound, because there is a virtuous circle at work: developing our friendships helps to strengthen our sense of self, which in turn helps to develop our friendships ... and so on.

But what we have always to bear in mind is that friendship is a mutual, reciprocal relationship. If there are things that we would like to get out of our friendship – including, but not only, a greater self-knowledge and a stronger sense of self – what are we prepared to put into it? The answer, I feel, is that we owe it to our friend to do what we can to encourage and support his or her self-knowledge and sense of self as well. This is to assume, of course, that that is what they themselves want, but I would question whether it is worth having the friendship of someone who finds their present state so perfectly satisfactory that they desire only to maintain it unchanged. If your friend is, like you, engaged on a quest for the rewards that a genuine friendship brings, he or she will welcome the encouragement and support that you give to their self-knowledge and sense of self. Fortunately your efforts and theirs will not only be mutually compatible but are bound to reinforce each other. As Robert Louis Stevenson put it, "It is only by trying to understand others that we can get our own hearts understood" (*Virginibus Puerisque*).

Our friendships join us to our friends in many ways: through doing things together, talking and listening to each other, giving and receiving; through trusting, caring and cherishing, accepting and respecting. And through all those links and connections, empathy too grows between us, and we jointly reaffirm each other's status as a free-standing individual in his or her own right.

Friendship is but one kind of relationship. It can't substitute for others: having friends is a different kind of experience from having a single, central partnership in one's life, for example. But by giving to our friendships our time and effort, our attention and devotion, by developing our ability to make and keep friends, we can discover within ourselves a capacity for rapport, for being at one with other people, that can make our lives very rewarding indeed.

Other Books

I have found the following books useful as sources of specific pieces of information or, more generally, in developing and clarifying my ideas about friendship. Where I have quoted directly from them in the text I have cited the writer and, on its first appearance, the title. However, the thinking of these writers, and indeed the thinking of writers whom they themselves were influenced by, has undoubtedly diffused into my own thinking and perspectives more broadly and deeply than those few quotations might suggest, and I take this opportunity to acknowledge my debt to them.

Argyle, Michael, *The Psychology of Interpersonal Behaviour* (4th edn), Harmondsworth, Penguin, 1983

Argyle, Michael, and Henderson, Monika, *The Anatomy of Relationships*, Harmondsworth, Penguin, 1985

Berger, John, *A Fortunate Man: The Story of a Country Doctor*, London, Allen Lane, 1967

Berne, Eric, *Games People Play*, London, Andre Deutsch, 1966

Bott, Elizabeth, *Family and Social Network* (2nd edn), London, Tavistock, 1957

Brown, Dennis, and Pedder, Jonathan, *Introduction to Psychotherapy*, London, Tavistock, 1979

Cartledge, Sue, and Ryan, Joanna (eds), *Sex and Love*, London, The Women's Press, 1983 (This contains contributions by Lynne Segal and Jill Brown, from which I have quoted.)

Chodorow, Nancy, *The Reproduction of Mothering*, Berkeley, Calif., University of California, 1978

Dickson, Anne, *A Woman In Your Own Right*, London, Quartet, 1982

Duck, Steve, *Friends, For Life*, Brighton, Harvester, 1983

Eichenbaum, Luise, and Orbach, Susie, *What Do Women Want?*, London, Fontana, 1984

Eichenbaum, Luise, and Orbach, Susie, *Understanding Women*, Harmondsworth, Penguin, 1985

Evison, Rose, and Horobin, Richard, *How To Change Yourself and Your World* (2nd edn), Sheffield, Co-counselling Phoenix (5 Victoria Rd, Sheffield), 1985

Gibran, Kahlil, *The Prophet*, London, Heinemann/Pan, 1926, republished 1980

Hardyment, Christina, *Dream Babies*, Oxford, Oxford University Press, 1984

Hodson, Phillip, *Men*, London, British Broadcasting Corporation, 1984

Ingham, Mary, *Men*, London, Century, 1984 (This is where I found the references to the books by Berger and Jourard.)

Jourard, Sidney, *The Transparent Self*, Princeton, N.J., Van Nostrand, 1964

Linehan, Marsha, and Egan, Kelly, *Asserting Yourself*, London, Century, 1983

McConville, Brigid, *Sisters*, London, Pan, 1985

Norwood, Robin, *Women Who Love Too Much*, London,

Arrow, 1986. *The* book on obsessive, compulsive love. It seems to strike a deep chord in many women.

Rowe, Dorothy, *Depression: The Way Out Of Your Prison*, London, Routledge & Kegan Paul, 1983 (This is where I found the references to Carol Parris's article and the quotation from Krishnamurti.)

Rubin, Lillian B., *Intimate Strangers*, New York, Harper & Row, 1983 (and republished in 1985 by Fontana, London)

Salmon, Phillida, *Living in Time*, London, Dent, 1985

Schiffman, Muriel, *Self Therapy*, Berkeley, Calif., Wingbow, 1967

Skynner, Robin, and Cleese, John, *Families and How to Survive Them*, London, Methuen, 1983

Spender, Dale, *Man Made Language* (2nd edn), London, Routledge & Kegan Paul, 1985

Storr, Anthony, *The Art of Psychotherapy*, London, Secker & Warburg/Heinemann, 1979

Tessina, Tina B., and Smith, Riley K., *How To Be A Couple And Still Be Free*, North Hollywood, Calif., Newcastle, 1980

Also available in Fount Paperbacks

The Mind of St Paul
WILLIAM BARCLAY

'There is a deceptive simplicity about this fine exposition of Pauline thought at once popular and deeply theological. The Hebrew and Greek backgrounds are described and all the main themes are lightly but fully treated.'   *The Yorkshire Post*

The Plain Man Looks at the Beatitudes
WILLIAM BARCLAY

'. . . the author's easy style should render it . . . valuable and acceptable to the ordinary reader.'   *Church Times*

The Plain Man Looks at the Lord's Prayer
WILLIAM BARCLAY

Professor Barclay shows how this prayer that Jesus gave to his disciples is at once a summary of Christian teaching and a pattern for all prayers.

The Plain Man's Guide to Ethics
WILLIAM BARCLAY

The author demonstrates beyond all possible doubt that the Ten Commandments are the most relevant document in the world today and are totally related to mankind's capacity to live and make sense of it all within a Christian context.

Ethics in a Permissive Society
WILLIAM BARCLAY

How do we as Christians deal with such problems as drug taking, the 'pill', alcohol, morality of all kinds, in a society whose members are often ignorant of the Church's teaching? Professor Barclay approaches a difficult and vexed question with his usual humanity and clarity, asking what Christ himself would say or do in our world today.